Notching Up

the NURTURED HEART APPROACH

The New Inner Wealth Initiative for Educators

WORKBOOK

the **NURTURED HEART APPROACH**

The New Inner Wealth Initiative
for Educators

WORKBOOK

by **Lisa Bravo**

with Howard Glasser and Melissa Lynn Block

the NURTURED HEART APPROACH

The New Inner Wealth Initiative for Educators

WORKBOOK

For information contact: Nurtured Heart Publications
4165 West Ironwood Hill Drive
Tucson, Arizona 85745
E-mail: adhddoc@theriver.com

For information about bulk purchasing discounts of this book or other Nurtured Heart Approach books, videos, CDs or DVDs, please contact Fulfillment Services at 800-311-3132. For orders within the book industry, please contact Brigham Distributing at 435-723-6611.

Heart paintings by Anne Labovitz

Book design by Richard Diffenderfer

Back cover design idea by Alice Glasser

Copy editing by Dreux Sutcliffe

Printed by Pollock Printing, Nashville, TN

Library of Congress Card Catalogue Number: Pending
ISBN 978-0-9826714-3-6
Printed in the United States
First Printing: January 2012

This book is dedicated to all educators
who light the way for our children.
Day after day, month after month, year
after year, and in the face of countless obstacles,
you relentlessly pursue your own greatness
and transform the lives of children.

Table of Contents

Acknowledgements

LIFE IS ABOUT THE JOURNEY, NOT THE DESTINATION. I know with all my heart that this journey, for me, is about bringing the Nurtured Heart message into the lives of children and the adults who care about them. This is a very important mission, and I've taken it on with all the reverence it requires. And as is the truth with any effort that matters, I haven't undertaken it alone.

To Melissa Block, steward of the approach and Nurtured Heart Tribe Scribe: Your gift with words and voice is tremendous! It has been a pleasure every step of the way. To my dear friend Howard Glasser: thank you for believing in me and for trusting me to help raise this baby! Thanks to Dreux Sutcliffe for his incisive proofreading and editing work. To all the teachers, children, and families who have endowed me with their trust: I am forever grateful.

Without the love, encouragement, support, and teamwork of my incredible family, I never would have tried this climb. David, my best other half, my rock and devoted husband: your greatness still takes my breath away. Thank you for always seeing the truth in each moment and for loving my intensity intensely!

To the young man I know as my baby Christopher: You impress me each day with your wisdom, humor, and integrity. Thank you for having such high standards for me as your mom. I have learned so much from you about how to be! To Danielle, my beautiful, wise, old soul: Your dreaming big inspires me every day. Thanks for being so clear and fearless about your path. I still hope to be you when I grow up.

—*Lisa Bravo*

Howard Glasser

THIS BOOK IS A DERIVATIVE of my early clinical work with difficult children. Our experience with the approach since its inception in the 1990s demonstrates that if it works for children who've been deemed impossible to reach, it will work wonders on any child. I'm especially grateful to the intense children who were instrumental in formulating this approach, and who continue to inspire my work every day. Their responsiveness to this approach has supported ongoing work towards making this an approach that is widely used for all children.

I continue to be amazed at all the groundbreaking work of so many dedicated people who continue to reveal new applications of the Nurtured Heart Approach with diverse groups of children, including those on the autism spectrum and in foster care. And this leads me to thank an amazing woman whose amazing mission has offered me the privilege of walking beside her, teaching with her, and collaborating with her on books like the one you are reading right now.

I am so grateful for Lisa Bravo showing up in my life as my dearest friend and colleague. She has generated so much brilliance and excitement for those learning, using and teaching Nurtured Heart Approach and in the adventure of bringing this approach to the world. I couldn't imagine a greater partner in this exciting journey. She has lit up the runway and engendered great hope for so many.

My great appreciation to Melissa Block who this time not only synthesized the words and thoughts of Lisa and I but whose contributions to the organization and writing of this volume are innumerable and vast. Her contributions and edits have made this volume clear, purposeful and accessible.

Thanks to Rich Diffenderfer for his graphic design artistry, which always yields an excellent interior and exterior style and look. Gratitude to greatness artist and Advanced Trainer Anne Leibovitz for the artwork that graces our cover.

So many thanks and great appreciation to the Advanced Trainers and practitioners of the Nurtured Heart Approach, who have become our family and friends and who keep us forever inspired with their amazing accomplishments. And great gratitude to my very own Nurtured Heart child, friend and teacher, Alice Glasser, my most important source of inspiration and love.

Are You Ready?

by Rhett Etherton

Rhett is a primary school teacher and Advanced Trainer of the Nurtured Heart Approach in the Phoenix, Arizona area. His work with students and colleagues is discussed at several points throughout this Workbook.

Think of that one intense student in your school who constantly seeks attention through breaking rules. Take a moment to really see that child in your mind's eye. Then, when I say, "Go!" I want you to list five great qualities of that student.

That's right. Five great qualities or, as you'll learn to refer to them, qualities of greatness. Expressions of that student's intrinsic greatness. No negative statements allowed. Recognize his or her greatness with all of your heart!

Are you ready? Set? All right…GO!

Was this task hard for you? If so, congratulations. You're ready to learn the Nurtured Heart Approach.

I've been using Howard Glasser's Nurtured Heart Approach in my elementary classroom to guide my interactions with students for five years, with great success. But just like a pitcher trying to perfect his curve ball or a guitar player trying to create new sounds with his guitar, I'm still looking for ways to notch it up. I'm always seeking ways to take my use of the approach to new levels: adding more heart to recognitions, becoming even more crystal clear about rules and consistent about consequences, and ensuring that all of my energy has been reallocated from misbehavior to greatness.

In his book Notching Up the Nurtured Heart Approach, Howard gave us specific techniques on how to deepen our practice of the approach. In this accompanying workbook by Lisa Bravo and Howard Glasser, we're guided further with interactive exercises and a fresh "Lisa-esque" spin on implementing Howard's ideas in the classroom.

The neat thing about this approach is that you can always notch it up! There will never be a point where you'll say, "Okay, I did all of these techniques. Things are good. I'm done!" You can always go deeper. The heart is integral to this approach, and is there really any end to the depth of the heart? Is there a set limit to the greatness a teacher or student can show? Strengthening and deepening your use of this approach will lead you and your class to greater levels of success!

When I first met Lisa Bravo, I was struggling to keep my head above water in my inner-city, English Language Learner classroom. How come my big smiles and my energetic choruses of "Thank you!" and "Good job!" weren't affecting my students? How come my stern lectures and negative phone calls home seemed to only make my intense students' behavior worse? At the time, I blamed myself! Nearly every day, I left work depressed and exhausted.

During one-on-one coaching, Lisa helped me by reflecting to me my own greatness as a teacher and by teaching me the techniques of the Nurtured Heart Approach. She taught me to notch it up by reflecting to me my own greatness as a teacher. Lisa guided me in taking consequences to a smarter, less energized level. I began to give a short, very low-energy consequence every time a rule was broken just a quick hand motion. Then, I learned to go right back to teaching nouns and celebrating the greatness of the children who weren't breaking the rules!

With Lisa's help, I converted my old, tired "Great job!" to something far more specific: "Victor, I really wish your mom could see you being an expert problem solver! She would be so proud!" I called students up to the front of the room after math lessons to give them a lecture...not about something that they did wrong, but about the great focus and determination they showed during their learning. I began showing video clips of my students I took during the lessons, then leading a class discussion of how the students in the videos were persevering and working hard. Less instructional time was wasted on misbehavior and students learned at faster rates. Yes, students continued to "act out," but now, they were acting out their greatness!

These results were wonderful, but it was time to notch it up...I was ready to transform my life! On my rides home from work, I began to list in my mind the greatness I showed that day. Whether I'd been confident enough to tell a fellow teacher I disagreed with her at a student's IEP (Individual Education Plan) meeting, or I was being loving to myself by taking a lunch break instead of working more on already great lesson plans, I found ways to energize myself for the greatness I was demonstrating.

I became an unstoppable force, energizing greatness everywhere I went. I energized the Wendy's drive-through worker: "I'm impressed that even though you guys are so busy, you are being so nice to people! I appreciate that!" I organized Nurtured Heart Happy Hours with my fellow teachers, where we would talk about the greatness we had shown that week. Notching up my own greatness (and that of others) gave me the balanced, happy, and peaceful life I have today.

Even though I've been using the approach for many years, been to numerous Advanced Trainings, and am even training and coaching others, I still find ways to notch it up every day. Currently, I'm working on something I call "instant forgiveness" in my class, where I strive to welcome a student from a reset with pure love with no residue of annoyance or anger about a rule having been broken.

In this book, Lisa will help you take your use of the approach to the next level. Are you ready to notch up the greatness of your students, your school...and yourself?

Ready...

set...

GO!

Preface

Life With a Transformed Child

Before having my own children, I was a therapist who worked with children and families. I studied all there was to study about parenting and taught parenting classes for ten years. My practice focused on very difficult children, many of whom had been abused. I was pretty sure I'd be a perfect mother.

My son Christopher changed all this.

As an infant, he wanted to nurse constantly. He never napped and slept poorly when he did sleep. When awake, he was constantly in motion and very prone to accidents. This boy was so active, so busy, that I quickly learned what it was to be frustrated enough as a parent to be capable of child abuse. I got how a child could drown in the tub while his mother was in the next room. And he was intense about it all, easily pushed into emotional states that disrupted the lives of everyone around him.

He was aggressive and didn't seem to understand how his body worked in spatial relationship to the bodies of other children. He'd go after a ball, knocking kids over in his wake; then he'd look back with an expression that said, "Why is everyone on the floor?" When I began to take him to play groups, he didn't get invited back.

To my relief, he did well in preschool. I volunteered there three or four times a week. But once he entered the highly structured Christian kindergarten program we thought would be the best fit for him, all hell broke loose. The third or fourth time the teacher called me, she was crying. She told Lisa that Christopher could not return to school until he was evaluated.

As a therapist, I knew these evaluations usually led to the prescription of medications like Ritalin. I knew my son could manage himself in certain settings. If he could do that, I reasoned, he must not have a disease that required medical intervention. I knew there had to be a way to help him manage himself better in all settings. And that's when I discovered the Nurtured Heart Approach.

As soon as I grasped the nature and foundations of this approach, I began to plug it in with my son, who by then had a younger sister, Danielle. Since then, it has changed everything about my parenting, as well as about my relationship with Christopher, Danielle and my husband. It gave me the tools I needed to be the mom I'd always thought I was going to be. Over time, I integrated the approach into my therapy practice and began to teach it to parents and educators.

I got to know Howard Glasser, the creator of the approach and the author of the book to which this workbook is a companion, and we began to give presentations together. We collaborated (with JoAnn Bowdidge) on a workbook for parents, which was published in 2007. Over the past four years, I have presented with Howard at the Advanced Trainings offered in Tucson, and presented on my own all over the U.S.

Here's what life is like with children who have been exposed to the Nurtured Heart Approach—at least, the children I've had the joy of mothering.

Christopher and Danielle were profoundly concerned about the damage Hurricane Katrina had done and about all the children who, in its aftermath, were homeless or couldn't find their parents. At the time, Christopher was in second grade and Danielle in first grade. Between them, they gathered kids on our street to form a "gang" called Carriage Way Kids' Coalition. They even had their own gang sign (a C and a W in sign language), which they flashed at cars as they drove by. (They live in Phoenix, Arizona, where gang violence is a significant concern.) They had clarity in their vision for the "gang" and were adamant they wanted to be "a gang that does great things."

The first thing the Carriage Way Kids' Coalition did was institute a penny drive to raise money for Katrina victims. Accompanied by parents, they swarmed along the street, bunching up on front porches, ringing doorbells, and hollering at whoever answered, "Can we have all your money for Katrina?" Once the parents helped them to ask more politely, they collected $500 to send to the Red Cross.

Their next project was to help a grandmother who was raising her seven grandchildren on her own on a nearby Indian reservation. They organized a gift drive for Christmas where people could drop off gifts and clothing. So much was collected that the parents had to rent a second van! Then, there was a book drive for our local domestic violence shelter; then, helping their mothers raise the several thousand dollars they needed to participate in the Three-Day Walk, a 60-mile fundraising walk in support of breast cancer research. They held a garage sale where they sold their own prized items to raise money. (Their sign initially said, "Raising Money for Breath Cancer.") Overall, they raised $4,000.

The Carriage Way Kids' Coalition went on for five years or so. Each of their projects came from their passionate curiosity and innate wisdom. They became very tuned in to the needs of others and learned how to actualize their collective understanding. Our local paper interviewed them.

At this writing, my son is 14 and just starting high school. Although I was concerned about his transition from a small, hands-on middle school where he was thriving to a typical high school setting, he is doing well. He loves it. He's learned how to love and embrace his intensity in remarkable ways.

His sister, Danielle, is also thriving. From a very early age, she has been acutely aware of the inequalities in our world. In 2010, she decided that she wants to become an attorney who "specializes in animal rights and in helping people who do not have a voice." She shared with us that she'd been researching law schools, and that she's concluded that Harvard Law is the best one. She is wise, intense, driven and focused in ways I never thought possible for a 12-year-old. I attribute this, and her brother's ability to thrive despite the challenges he faced in younger years, to their having been exposed to the Nurtured Heart approach since they were very young.

Christopher and Danielle embody a basic truth about children who are raised in this approach. They consistently demonstrate something we call inner wealth. Those who have inner wealth move through the world with an acute awareness and consciousness. Because they have a firm grounding in their own greatness, they are free to put their energy into a passionate curiosity about the world around them. Because of this groundedness, they aren't needy, so they can readily give to others.

Kids with inner wealth want to share and collaborate with others around them. They are kind, collaborative, respectful, confident, and resistant to negative peer pressure. They are aware that they are here for a higher purpose. Clarity of intention, clarity about the divine order of things, and concern about values alignment are integral parts of who they are. The transformed child is tuned into his or her own needs. At school, the transformed child does not need to be micromanaged or controlled. She wants to do her work, and she knows that her effort to do it well is what matters most not the numbers on her report card or her scores on tests.

Christopher's intensity has not gone away, but he has learned how to handle and channel it into positive actions and intentions. He took up hockey, where he can be physical according to the rules and where the strict structure of those rules puts him in the penalty box when he crosses the line. At home, he heads out to the trampoline to burn off excess energy.

This approach has helped Christopher to purposefully and actively create his concept of self from a place of love and acceptance. He has learned to value his quirkiness as a unique gift. He embraces his intensity, regulating it to match the needs of most any situation. He's conscious about modulating his intensity when it builds up.

When Danielle started out in middle school, she had difficulty adjusting. I tried coaching her a little about making friends. "Mom," she said, "I'm not going to just make friends with someone so I don't have to sit alone at lunch. It has to be someone who has an impact on my life."

"Danielle, when I grow up, I want to be just like you," I answered. Smiling gently, she said, "It's okay. You're getting there. Just love yourself through it."

At this writing, Danielle had just made a very important decision to move from her current school, where she does not feel academically challenged, to a school with a more rigorous curriculum. What 12-year-old does that? We didn't push her in any way in this direction; she just has high standards for herself. She's fearless in her efforts to manifest her greatest self. We're just along for the ride!

In my career as a family psychotherapist, I have taught thousands of families how to implement the Nurtured Heart Approach. I've has found that the intrinsic self-worth and internalized greatness that emerged in my children in response to this approach is not the exception; it's the rule. This is the case not only for children, but for adults who learn and apply the approach with children in their lives. Even when it is applied minimally, parents and educators report significant results.

This approach is a powerful social-emotional curriculum that goes beyond consequences and rules. Traditional parenting and teaching methods typically come from a reactive framework, responding to poor behavior and broken rules with a punishment or a consequence designed to teach a lesson. The Nurtured Heart Approach proactively super-energizes successes in real time, creating an experience of connectedness around those moments of success. These experiences of authentic connection change the landscape of both the parent-child relationship and the child's subjective experience of success. A sense of intrinsic value and self-worth is cultivated.

It begins not by telling children how they ought to "be respectful…be kind…be helpful" but by purposefully creating and modeling a way of relating that acknowledges and appreciates children for the many good choices and qualities that already exist in them and in their lives. At the same time, the reward of energized, intense connection around rule-breaking and falling short of expectations is curtailed. The approach dramatically changes the way energy flows within the relationship between adult and child.

At Tolson Elementary in Tucson, Arizona, the approach has been used school-wide since 1999, thanks to the courage of principal Maria Figueroa in mandating its school-wide application. Tolson is a Title 1 school of over 500 children, 80 percent of whom qualify for free or reduced lunch. Before the Nurtured Heart Approach, Tolson had eight times the normal number of school suspensions per year than other schools in the district. Many were referred for ADHD assessments and put on medications. Teacher attrition was well over 50 percent per year.

Since Nurtured Heart, no children at all have been diagnosed with ADHD and no additional children were placed on medications. Special education utilization has dropped from 15 percent to one percent, while the Gifted and Talented program has expanded from less than five percent of students to over 15 percent! Best of all, the school's standardized test scores have gone from the worst in the district to rank among the best. Positive progress has been dramatic and continuous. Teacher attrition has fallen to nearly zero, and teachers don't call in sick on Fridays or Mondays nearly as often. Student attendance is also dramatically higher.

We've heard many more success stories and promising statistics on achievement, reduced disciplinary referrals and other improvements with the Nurtured Heart Approach: from Cooley Middle School in Roseville, California; Rocky River Elementary in Monroe, North Carolina; the Intergenerational School in Cleveland, Ohio; and a growing number of other schools, early childhood education centers, foster care agencies, and 'boot camp' programs for troubled children.

Data collection is ongoing at many of these schools, and the numbers are amazing. At Michelson Elementary in California, for example, the Nurtured Heart Approach brought a 20 percent drop in disciplinary infractions, a 50 percent decrease in chronic truancy, and a 27 percent drop in office referrals over a one-year period. At North Education Center, a high-level special education school near Minneapolis, Minnesota, principal Amy Sward reports that the number of prone restraints fell from 22 in the first week of school to two in the first month following school-wide implementation in 2011. (You'll hear more about Amy's experience, in her own words, in Chapter Nine.) We are compiling data to make the Nurtured Heart Approach evidence-based by the end of 2012.

Wherever this model is used, transformation happens. It happens in the people with whom you consciously, intentionally use it. And we hope that learning and applying this approach is transformative for you as well.

Introduction

Into the Abyss

We can't solve problems by using the same kind of thinking we used when we created them.

— Albert Einstein

In all my years of working with educators, no teacher has reported to me that the aim of getting into that line of work had to do with generous pay, fame or glory. As teachers, they are fulfilling a special calling.

After parents and caregivers, teachers are the most important adults in the lives of children. They have the profound ability to change the course of a child's life through teacher-student interactions. Over the past decade, I've had the honor and privilege of teaching hundreds of educators to implement the Nurtured Heart Approach in the classroom setting. Their willingness to do everything in their power to improve the lives of children never fails to inspire me.

If you are a teacher, you have been put on this earth to change the world. At the same time, you have chosen a very demanding profession. In my therapy practice, teachers often seek me out for psychotherapeutic support because they're stressed, anxious or depressed. I've come to know one thing for certain: that teaching has the potential to be one of the most draining and thankless jobs in the workplace today.

It is estimated that one in every two teachers will leave the profession within the first three years in the field.[1] Many who end up learning the Nurtured Heart Approach are teachers who feel ill-equipped to handle the everyday challenges of managing negative behaviors in the classroom.

Teachers are under intense scrutiny. They are expected to get students to perform academically, and they have little time to cope with discipline problems. Ironically, they report spending countless hours implementing the discipline policies of their classrooms which, often, includes teaching the class in great detail about the meaning of each rule and what happens if you break the rule, while including some sort of character education. Beyond this implementation, teachers often need some way of tracking behavior, as well as writ-

1. National Education Association: www.all4ed.org/files/archive/publications/TeacherAttrition.pdf

ing behavioral plans for students. No wonder they become frustrated when all this work yields minimal (if any) effect on students. All the while, they're desperately trying to remain faithful to the theories and practices they studied at their respective schools of education.

Teachers report feeling overwhelmed and out of gas. When they first hear about the Nurtured Heart Approach many are skeptical…and rightly so! Who wants yet another classroom management program passed along to them as a "positive behavioral approach" but that might still be, at its core, just another punitive approach to gaining control over the challenging child in the classroom? The NHA is not behavior management; nor is it based on gaining external control over children by wielding adult authority. Nurtured Heart boils down to creating connected, powerful, healthy relationships.

This approach helps build a positive, helpful, loving, non-confrontational culture in the school setting and creates a new classroom culture by changing how students and educators see each other. It's not just about following steps designed to modify student behavior; it's about educators learning to tune into the gifts and great qualities of students and of themselves. This creates a culture of greatness, which then trickles down in unexpected and magical ways.

In order for students to be available for learning, they must first have a sense of social and emotional safety and competence. Once this is achieved, the child is able to process and retain cognitive learning at a higher rate.[2] The Nurtured Heart Approach is an ideal tool for building this kind of safety and sense of competence in the classroom. Leaders in the field of social-emotional learning and in the realm of resiliency have placed high priority on relationship in the big picture of creating strong learners. Research on the importance of connectedness has drawn very similar conclusions, demonstrating that higher levels of student connectedness lead to better educational outcomes. Some of the leaders in these fields have come to view the Nurtured Heart Approach as an optimal way to create connected, aligned, powerful relationship.

This approach asks teachers to take the lead in transforming negativity. It asks them to shift from a perspective of scarcity to a perspective of abundance; to shift from a notion of instilling information to one of recognizing students for the innate, unique forms of intelligence they already possess—the intelligences that allow them to learn in their own ways. It teaches educators to see students as having everything they need when they come in, as opposed to seeing, identifying, and fixing deficits.

---

2. danielgoleman.info/topics/social-emotional-learning/

With this approach, the educator's job becomes one of helping students to actualize what they already possess. Teaching becomes a matter of relating to students most intimately and energetically around this process of positive self-actualization. When teachers have addressed the social and emotional needs of the students in their classrooms, they create a culture where students are intrinsically motivated.

When I consult with schools, I'm often asked, "What's the curriculum for this approach?" Most educators want a concrete, meaningful, stepwise way to implement the tools of the approach, and this workbook is my attempt to provide just that with support and contributions from Howard Glasser, the creator of the Nurtured Heart Approach.

If you are a teacher, this book is designed to help you create the classroom you've always wanted and provide tools and ideas for learning that you may not have considered so far.

If you are an administrator, you can use this learning to help you lead schools or districts into a cultural shift that will create legacies for all children served there.

If you are a school counselor, you will find powerful new ways to connect with students. You may find yourself particularly challenged by the foundations of this approach, but know that it can enable a shift from a place of dealing only with crises or trying to prevent them to one of creating successes at every turn. Often, in schools where this approach is implemented, school counselors find that their role shifts from one of putting out fires to one of inspiring and supporting staff members in cultivating greatness in students and each other. This role is often key to whole-school success.

If you are a parent, you will learn the most recent iteration of this approach here and in the companion book. You'll gain a perspective that reaches across both home and school. In the context of this approach, parents can see the beauty of purposeful intention to embrace a greatness mindset at home and at school.

If you are a certified Advanced Trainer of the Nurtured Heart Approach, you will also find this book (and its companion volume) useful in furthering your knowledge and skill in working with educators, parents and others. You'll find powerful new ways of creating shift in systems, policies and culture through those you are training in this approach. Trainers can get stuck in ways of coaching educators that are all about solving specific problems:

"What if this particular scenario happens in my classroom?"

"What about this particular child who doesn't seem to want to come around?"

"How do I deal with this child who seems to be escalating unwanted behaviors in response to the approach?"

Although it's done with the best of intentions, this kind of troubleshooting runs counter to the deepest tenets of this approach, which tell us to shift the focus from problems to greatness. Through the Notching Up the Nurtured Heart Approach book and workbook, trainers will learn to stop troubleshooting and putting out fires. Instead, they'll build tools for giving trainees everything they need to solve their own problems. The classroom activities in this book provide ideas for weaving the approach into daily school life in expansive and pragmatic ways with the intention of bringing the Nurtured Heart Approach to life in the classroom.

Since starting to work in schools in 2003, I've seen that this approach's methods run counter to what most educators have learned about classroom management and ways of interacting with students. Resistance is common, especially in the early phases of learning about and implementing the approach. When you run up against your own resistance, we hope you will have the faith to embrace and implement the counterintuitive methods described here and in the companion book.

Are you reading this book because you are desperately searching for something that will change the way you currently feel about teaching? As the parent of a formerly difficult and intense child, I know what desperation feels like. Howard told me, just as he's told many other parents, "Do the approach like your life depends on it; then, you'll see transformation." I did exactly that: I applied the approach as though my life depended on it, and it made all the difference for me and my family. It's a leap of faith to try something that goes against everything you currently know about what drives the emotional lives of children. But if you have read this far, chances are you are ready for a drastic change in your teaching life and in the many lives you touch each day.

See this book as the roadmap for the adventure of a lifetime—a hero's journey into the unknown! A new way of thinking always feels scary and strange at first. Embrace your fears, skepticism, and resistance and use the energy of these experiences as your jet fuel to create a new trajectory for your life. Challenge yourself to take the leap of trusting the approach, and you'll find miraculous changes on the other side of that void.

I've come to the frightening conclusion that I am the decisive element in the classroom.

It's my daily mood that makes the weather.

As a teacher, I possess a tremendous power to make a child's life miserable or joyous.

I can be a tool of torture or an instrument of inspiration.

I can humiliate or humor, hurt or heal.

In all situations, it is my response that decides whether a crisis will be escalated or de-escalated and a child humanized or dehumanized.

—Haim Ginott

Ginott, Haim. *Between Parent and Child: The Bestselling Classic That Revolutionized Parent-Child Communication*; Three Rivers Press, 2003.

Chapter One

On Greatness

THE WORD "GREATNESS" HAS ALREADY APPEARED IN THIS BOOK SEVERAL TIMES. How has it struck you so far? Does it resonate with you…or does it freak you out a little?

What does greatness mean to you? Can you see it in others? Do you see it in yourself? Does the notion that you are great bring up resistance, or does greatness feel like something with which you are aligned? Or are you totally comfortable with seeing others as great while stopping short of attributing greatness to yourself?

Teachers tend to evaluate with a critical eye. The methods they learn in their own education generally focus on getting as much as possible out of students, which usually involves focusing on gaps and shortfalls and pouring energy into solving problems. This discerning, critical focus teachers cultivate often gets turned back on themselves.

Many of the clients I see in my private therapy practice are teachers who are very good at seeing what's wrong—how not great everything is. They end up struggling against anxiety and depression because their ideas about what should be (and isn't) trump their appreciation for gifts and strengths. In theory and philosophy, these people often believe themselves to be highly positive; but in day-to-day, minute-to-minute, moment-to-moment life, where the rubber meets the road, an underlying negativity often runs the show.

Before we get into the meaning of greatness in Nurtured Heart terms, write down your own thoughts and feelings around greatness in the space provided below.

Notching it Up!

What are your "gut" thoughts and feelings about the word ***greatness****? Don't over-think; just write the first thing that comes to you and keep writing until you run out of space.*

In the Nurtured Heart Approach, this word takes on new depth and breadth. Here, greatness is something everyone possesses. It's endowed to each of us because we exist in this world. Any positive quality that can be discerned is an expression of that greatness.

Greatness is the energy that dances and shines within each of us just because we're alive. In the Nurtured Heart context, it has nothing to do with the energy of conceit, self-righteousness, or entitlement. We use this word to convey the pure light that every human being possesses; no one has more than anyone else. Qualities like honesty, respectfulness, creativity, compassion, courage, cooperativeness or passion are expressions of this inner greatness.

In reflecting greatness to children, we demonstrate that life's rewards are more abundant when they choose to accept their own greatness and live into it fully. We show them, both through our own example and through the ways we relate to them, that their greatness is a given. They can choose to live lives that are about cultivating and expanding this greatness.

A Spiritual Practice

Some think of the Nurtured Heart Approach as just a behavioral intervention and a social-emotional curriculum. Although these are crucial and important ways of defining its impact in schools, it goes far beyond these definitions. It is, essentially, a spiritual practice. As a spiritual practice, it is compatible with every faith and tradition, or it can stand on its own.

In this context, spirituality is about an awakening to the inner workings of the soul or life force. It is about learning to see and feel that greatness is something shared by every human being, and that no person possesses more intrinsic greatness than any other person. It's a shared entity. Some just need more help bringing it out than others.

We call the Nurtured Heart Approach a spiritual practice because it isn't just about changing what you do, or even the way you think. The focus of this approach is on opening the heart. When the heart opens to change, the brain will follow, and you will make new, heart-centered choices in your relationships with students (and other people!). You can learn and apply this approach without opening your heart, but it will be more difficult, and you won't be as effective.

What exactly does this mean, to open one's heart? It isn't something that can be understood intellectually; it has to be felt and experienced. Try this exercise to begin to get a taste of this opening.

Notching it Up!

Sit comfortably. Bring your attention to the very center of your chest, where an imaginary line between the collarbones and the base of the center of the ribcage and your left and right shoulders would intersect. Allow this center of attention to extend the full depth of the chest from front to back. This is the heart center, also known as the heart chakra. It's a central energetic "hub" in the human body.

Close your eyes and take a few slow, even breaths in and out, imagining that the breath is moving in and out of that heart center. Stay with it until you begin to feel something shifting or expanding in your body. Journal your experience below.

Did you feel an expansion? A warmth? A sense of compassion or love? This is the experience of being in the heart. Being able to tune into that heart frequency helps immeasurably in successfully implementing this approach. When children perceive that they are being approached in this manner, and when they process their experience through a heart-centered lens of greatness, they are more open and receptive to learning. And they learn this through the example of adults who interact with them through the same heart-centered lens.

At this point, your mind may have wandered to thoughts such as: "Does staying in my heart and seeing only greatness mean that we just let them get away with it when they do something wrong?" No! For now, hold that question and trust that it will be answered in much more detail in coming chapters.

Aligning With Greatness

The work of the Nurtured Heart Approach is to find ways to see and eloquently describe positive qualities as evidence of the larger greatness in ourselves and in those with whom we interact. As we cultivate this ability, we find that giving energy to greatness causes it to grow, expand and take on new dimensions. **Greatness is not the opposite of anything; it's all-encompassing.** Qualities like focus, respectfulness, desire to do things well, cooperativeness, truthfulness, or generosity spring from this foundation of greatness.

This process begins with developing the ability to see and describe each person's intrinsic greatness and its many expressions. **When you reflect greatness to a child, the child begins to act out greatness.** In the simplest terms, this is accomplished by recognizing students in vivid verbal detail whenever they are: 1.) doing something right; or 2.) not doing something wrong.

You may have heard of research demonstrating that too much praise is bad for children. A closer look at that research, however, shows that the amount of praise isn't the problem; it's the kind of praise given. To effectively improve a child's self-image, praise has to be given in a certain way. In the Nurtured Heart Approach, we avoid confusion on this point by using words like acknowledge, recognize, appreciate or energize rather than praise.

As you learn Nurtured Heart tools for acknowledging, accepting and seeing the greatness in your students, you will become more skilled at seeing and describing it in other people around you, including colleagues, family members, even strangers...and (last, but definitely not least) in yourself.

Aligning with greatness is about seeing miracles everywhere because that's how you choose to see things. It's about aligning with ourselves and our own fundamental internal wisdom and appreciating how that wisdom exists and is expressed in others.

Now that you have a better grasp of the Nurtured Heart definition of greatness, consider: how and in what ways do you align with your own greatness? When someone compliments you, do you become uncomfortable? Where do you have trouble with this?

Notching it Up!

Try describing some qualities of your own greatness. What are your gifts? What are your talents? How do you shine? What qualities of greatness do you wish you had more of?

How does it feel to you to write about yourself in this way? What does it bring up for you?

Think of a friend, relative, celebrity, statesperson or other person you respect and admire. What qualities of theirs do you wish you had more of yourself?

If you're like most people new to this approach, you have some trouble finding words to describe positive qualities. By the time you finish this book, you'll have far greater resources on that front.

If you didn't come up with much of a testimony to your own greatness here, consider this: you possess at least a glimmer of any quality of greatness you can discern in someone else. The process of learning this approach will bring you to see greatness in ways and places where you've never looked before, as well as giving you tools you can use to speak eloquently and honestly about that greatness.

You can learn and use the Nurtured Heart Approach without appreciating your own greatness, but it will be harder, and you won't be as effective in applying it to your students. You may as well give it a shot.

Notching it Up!

Re-consider each quality you admire in another person. Write that quality down, and then write down some way—even if it's very, very small—that you have expressed that quality yourself, or a way in which you are expressing it right now. ***If you can see it in someone else, you possess it! If you didn't, you would not have the capacity to notice it in another.***

For example: if you see a quality of courageousness in someone else, you might see yourself as lacking that quality. Re-frame this by finding even a glimmer of courage or a movement in that direction and calling yourself out for that expression of courage: "Today I was feeling nervous about making that phone call but I went ahead and did it. That was courageous of me."

The What and the How

This workbook is designed to teach you how to create a culture of greatness in the classroom. The approach's techniques will enable you to demonstrate that greatness exists in each moment. As you learn to apply these techniques to students, you will be encouraged to apply them to yourself as well.

Nurtured Heart is a practice, just like yoga or meditation. It begins with cultivating awareness of the way you automatically think about the world and how you relate to others. Finding fault, ruminating on worry or fear, being critical, and seeing what's wrong can be what Howard calls a "default mode," and as you learn this approach, you will come to see that this default can be changed if you wish to change it. From there, the practice is about gently changing course and grounding in the moment to see what's right, what's good, and what's great on a daily, hourly, moment-to-moment basis.

Most of what you'll learn in the chapters to come is about the "what" of this approach: the language, the stands, the intentions, the techniques, the underlying concepts. We all know what it's like to try to start something new in our lives: change a bad habit, for example, or improve our diets, or to exercise regularly. We set out to do this with full intellectual understanding of what to do and why it's important…only to find ourselves falling off the wagon yet again. How do we move into a new way of being and relating?

If what you learn in this book is something you wish to put into action, but you find that the *how* is much harder than the *what*, enlist others to support you. Talk to others about what you're doing and provide support and encouragement to those who find this path as exciting as you do. Know that this isn't about perfection, or even about getting it right all the time. A big part of learning this approach is learning to stay in the moment and quickly get back on track when you revert to old ways of relating to students.

This approach is not an intellectual approach, so looking at it through an intellectual framework will likely hold you back. Traditional methods are essentially extrinsic, but here, we need to shift to a mindset that is intrinsically based: heart-centered. Challenge yourself to process the information you learn in this workbook from your heart, through an emotional lens.

Don't let "the G-word" scare you. Use it often, starting now. Let it be a cue to move you into your heart. In chapters to come, you'll learn how to bring your own creative spin, unique personality and energy to this culture of greatness you're creating.

Start out with this experiment to help you grasp how powerful this word can be.

Notching it Up!

Silently make a statement of your greatness. Try: "I have the greatness of being thoughtful and caring," or something more general like, "I am great greatness."

Repeat this several times. How does this feel? Check in with body sensations, in particular. Do you feel any physical shifts?

The next time you are around others, whether they're your family, your colleagues or your students, look around and tell yourself silently something specific or general about the greatness you see: "They have the greatness of being consistent and reliable" or "We are great greatness."

Repeat your chosen phrase several times. What do you notice in yourself?

____

____

____

____

____

____

Now, let's move on to the nuts and bolts of the approach that will support you in making your praises highly specific in their references to greatness.

Chapter Two

Meltdowns or Mastery: *You Decide!*

Think back to a moment when a child in your care began to spin out of control. If you work with young children or special-needs children, this might look like a tantrum gathering momentum. If you work with middle-schoolers or teens, you might imagine a child refusing to comply with rules or requests, cursing, threatening, destroying property or hurting someone else—which is, in the end, really just another form of tantrum.

No matter what the age of the child or the form in which the meltdown appears, the adult's response tends to include some variation on the themes of helplessness, fear and anger. The amplitude of this response and the success with which the adult is able to table those feelings and handle the situation appropriately tends to vary depending on other factors, including what kind of day the educator has had.

Notching it Up!

Recall your own experience with difficult children: your most horrifying classroom or parenting experience; imagine the child you just could not handle despite your best efforts; the child you wish you could have rescued but couldn't.

This will be your only chance in this entire workbook to rant, complain, point fingers, and focus on negativity and problems, so go ahead: let it rip!

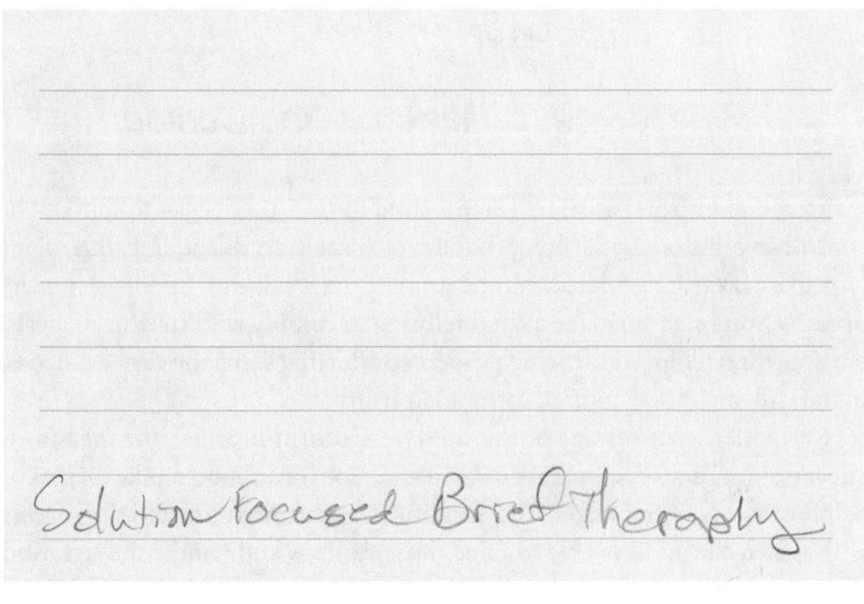

Now, check in with how you are feeling.

Did ranting about these problems make you feel better? Relieve any stress or strain? Or do you feel as tense, wound-up, and frustrated as you did in those moments you described in your journaling? More so?

Many hold a belief that this kind of venting helps improve our situations, but the ground truth doesn't support this conclusion. Although we might claim that we want to stay positive, we're feeding exactly the thing we don't want by focusing our energy on it.

Notching it Up!

In the situation described in Part I, what values did you uphold in spite of your frustrations? Were you patient? Did you refrain from losing your self-control? Did you do your best to regain your composure and start over? Did you experience the greatness of your determination, tenacity, or deep caring? In what other ways did you succeed in this difficult situation?

Upside-Down Energy

The key to shifting the dynamic from meltdowns to mastery is understanding the reasons why children melt down.

Most methods of positive discipline state that children act out because they have unmet needs. They're unable to communicate those needs, and so they act out. In most approaches, adults are advised to try to figure out what these unmet needs might be and to try to meet them. At that point, ideally, the child no longer feels the need to act out. The Nurtured Heart Approach reduces all unmet student needs into one simple common denominator: the need for energized connection with the most important person in the room. (That's you.)

Notching it Up!

Describe your current teaching style and approach to discipline. Is it a unified approach you learned in a class or from a book? Have you cobbled together elements of various approaches that resonate with you? How is your current approach working?

*The purpose of this exercise is to understand the differences between what you **have** been doing and what you **will** be doing. There are no wrong answers here. No adult who seeks to learn this approach* *is to blame for having used methods that aren't a good match for intense children. If what you've been doing isn't working, the methods are the problem. Normal classroom methods don't take the energetic truth of relationship into account.*

Learning approach description:

What do you think is working?

What do you think is not working?

Chances are, you just described a formulation from the vantage points of classroom management, expectations, rules and discipline policies. While these are all necessary ingredients of a successful classroom, one crucial link in the formula often goes unexamined:

Relationship!

The Nurtured Heart Approach is founded in an idea of relationship as an energetic exchange. Our words might say one thing, but when the energetic truth of relationship contradicts those words, energy runs the show. This approach gives tools for changing the way energy flows between adults and children. For a moment, step back from standard ideas about discipline and consider this.

Most of those who turn to this approach are dealing with some level of out-of-the-box intensity from students. Many teachers will tell you that schools are home to increasing numbers of children who act out in outrageous ways—children we like to call "high rollers." Many teachers feel unprepared for the intensity of many of the children who cycle through their classrooms. They are frustrated at having to spend so much energy and time just keeping the room under control.

Think about what happens when a child acts out. The teacher does her best to ignore and redirect. The intense child continues to up the ante to the point where the teacher must stop the lesson and deliver a consequence to the child. This is usually some version of turning a name card, losing points or taking something away. This is enough to get the average child to change his behavior, but if I'm the high roller, this encourages me to keep testing the teacher to see just how much energy I can get channeled in my direction. Eventually, the disruption gets to the point where the teacher must get involved in bigger, juicier ways. At this point, the child receives some form of energized lecture or caring concern; and he's probably also being energized by his peers for his behavior.

The high roller gets focused attention, relationship and connection in exchange for pushing boundaries or breaking rules. It might be a form of relationship that seems positive (focused time with the child to investigate the child's unmet need, or the giving of some form of extra support in the midst of a problem) or negative ("Quit it!" "Stop it!" "If you don't knock that off RIGHT NOW I'll..." or a long, loud lecture), but either way, it's energized. It's more.

Let's say you're having a terrible day and lack the patience to stick to your positive discipline guns. On a better day, a child's acting-out might have led to a persuasive discussion or shared words of wisdom: a heartfelt, calm and compassionate attempt to meet the child's unmet needs. But when you're at your ragged edge, this same situation launches you straight into warnings or, perhaps, into even more energized responses like yelling, nagging, threats, or lectures.

Meanwhile, the child is experiencing the energetic truth of what is going on. Even though she is being urged toward good choices, she recognizes that her experience of relationship with you is pale when she complies. When she makes a poor choice, the energy is strong, present and excited. **As the child encounters the truth of how energy flows, she comes to feel more celebrated and loved** when things are going wrong.

Let Go of All Other Approaches...At Least For Now

We're going to request here that you do something that might, at first, seem crazy. Abandon all other approaches—at least until you've tried this one, lock, stock and barrel. Let go of every notion you hold about how to discipline children and fully turn toward the new way described in this book.

People often try to implement this approach while continuing to hold allegiances to other approaches that feed upside-down energy. Or their own conditioning and upbringing keep them allied to an upside-down dynamic. They are probably not going to get the results they seek.

This approach is self-contained and comprehensive. It works best when used on its own, letting go of any attachment to other approaches. If you continue to give energy to negativity while trying to implement this new approach, your efforts to implement the Nurtured Heart Approach will be undermined.

Consider what happens when this same child is being "good" or not breaking any rules. What does he get? Not much. Maybe he hears something like "Good job!" or "Thanks for sitting quietly," but these non-specific praises fail to deliver anything near the intensity of relationship the child gets when acting out. Intense children have multiple experiences that reinforce the belief that they get more out of adversity.

I remember testing this many times in my early career as an intense and difficult child. I would try my hardest to follow directions, sit still, raise my hand, and "be good." Often, my teachers would be pleased and leave me alone so that nothing would interfere with the streak of good behavior that was making room for me to learn academically. But being good demanded a lot of my energy and concentration, and I soon found that it made me invisible. I perceived that the only way to be truly seen was to act out.

Again: traditional approaches tend to give more of our energy, our life force, our attention and focus to children when they are breaking rules or threatening to break rules than we give when they are being good. When things are going well, many of us tend to take a few steps back to avoid disrupting the lovely picture we see before us...and maybe to get a few things done while all is peaceful in the classroom!

Most of us also tend to energize negativity in our interactions with other adults and in the way we talk to ourselves. We can easily be drawn to conflict, drama and difficulty. We can wax poetic when talking about problems, but we rarely talk to children with the same sort of elaborate eloquence about what is going right or when things are going well. And how often do we get excited about what could be going wrong…but isn't?

People are generally positive when things are going well. But when "the rubber meets the road," we get to see how truly positive (or negative) we are. Even when we aren't hard on others, many of us have an unconscious habit of criticizing, blaming or mocking ourselves whenever the slightest thing goes wrong. The needle of awareness can get stuck in that groove. For some, it stays there for a lifetime.

Notching it Up!

Think about a recent time when you felt you'd done something wrong or behaved in a way you regretted. Write down the way you talked to yourself about it in the aftermath, or the way you related the story to someone else.

Notice whether your self-talk was critical. Consider: would you ever talk in this way to a cherished loved one or someone you admired? To a colleague? To a student? If you criticized yourself harshly, in extensive detail, consider: Would you ever criticize someone else in this way?

Re-read what you wrote above. Now, look at what went well. Identify the goodness and greatness that happened in those moments.

The request in this last exercise was challenging. You may have struggled to discern the positive in what you identified as your darkest moment. Congratulations on seeing what went right and putting it down on the page. You're demonstrating perseverance and a willingness to think outside the box. Even in considering a response, you're being thoughtful and engaged—both great qualities.

Now. Read your re-frame out loud. Notice how your voice adopts a new cadence, tone and expression when you are seeing yourself in greatness. Notice what a difference this makes in how the whole exchange feels. Notice how it feels to intentionally create the way you communicate. Does it feel uncomfortable? Or does it feel as though you are simply taking on the role of screenwriter and director in the movie that is your life—a role you've always had (at least, since you became an adult) but may not have truly owned until this moment?

Yes: you are the creator, producer, editor and director of each moment. You decide what you will 'film': what footage is important, where you wish to zoom in on details, and where you take the broad view.

Just as you can choose to take time to see and appreciate what children are doing right, you can choose to see and appreciate yourself for what YOU are doing right. You can choose to recognize the fact that things go right far more than they go wrong, even on the worst nightmare of a day.

Sounds simple, right? Just plug it in and go?

If you are a skeptic like me, you know that implementing simple concepts in real life can be a messy process. If I had a dime for every time a parent or teacher came to me and said that implementing this approach is "hard" or noticing what's going well is "exhausting," I would be a very wealthy woman. Changing patterns is a huge undertaking. It requires total commitment simply to reach the point where we break the bonds of habit and fully realize that we have a choice. We don't have to water weeds.

Learning to do this requires:

1. a major shift in intention, where we make a pledge to ourselves to start tuning in to what's right instead of what's wrong; and

2. purposeful implementation of specific techniques of the approach that allow us to put this intention into practice.

Upside-Down Energy

Howard often says that giving our energy and relationship when things are going wrong is like telling the child, "Oops, broke a rule…here's 100 bucks!" Nobody would do this on purpose, but almost everyone (accidentally) does it energetically. **When we give our energy to what we don't want, we're handing out $100 bills for negative or unwanted behavior.** The stands, intentions and techniques of the approach are intended to work interdependently, and are designed to turn upside-down energy right side up: to give energetic hundred-dollar bills in exchange for what we do want.

Clarity and purpose about where you spend your energy in the classroom changes the ways in which you spend your time and energy among your colleagues. You refrain from water cooler meltdowns, drama-laden meetings and toxic teacher luncheons. You shift conversations to identifying and celebrating greatness. You become warrior-like in your passion for celebrating your greatness, the greatness of your coworkers and the greatness of your students.

Responding to Resistance

First they laugh at you, then they fight you, then you win.

— Mahatma Gandhi

Are you experiencing what we call the "Yeah, but…" factor?

"Yeah, but you don't know the kids I have to deal with…"

"Yeah, but I have so many things to accomplish in a day, and energizing kids is just one more…"

"Yeah, but you aren't a teacher, Lisa Bravo—so you don't have any idea how hard my job is!"

This is your own resistance coming to the surface. Acknowledge it, embrace it, and use the energy of your resistance to get YOU clearer about what you are fighting for!

As you grow and evolve this approach, some of your friends and colleagues will be all-in and some will be resistant. You might be on an island of your own for a while, but eventually others will buy in. Resistance becomes toxic only when we see it as negative.

Whatever its source, embrace resistance and **view it simply as energy flowing in the wrong direction**. Know that you don't need to avoid the energy of resistance. See it as an energy, plain and simple, without judging it as good or bad. Embrace its energy and use it to get clearer, stronger, and more purposeful in the way you channel it. Use that energy as fuel for your determination to move into even more greatness.

In the years I've spent coaching teachers, I've heard every "Yeah, but…" at least once, and I've seen them all fall by the wayside once a commitment is made to flip upside-down energy right-side up. It's especially fun to see those questions dissolve in the days following the flip. Teachers become confident, amazed and exhilarated as they understand their new level of impact.

Right-Side-Up Energy Creates Inner Wealth

The purpose of the Nurtured Heart Approach is the cultivation of inner wealth. Inner wealth encompasses self-esteem and self-confidence, but goes beyond these characteristics. It is the purest part of who we are, transmitted through our visions of ourselves and of others, and how we interact in the world.

A child with inner wealth feels capable of living a life of greatness. In turn, she readily sees the greatness in other people. Inner wealth helps children handle strong feelings, remain grounded and present in difficult situations, and gravitate to peers and adults who will support them in greatness. A child with inner wealth wants to make positive choices and interact with others in positive ways.

Development of inner wealth corresponds with development of an internal locus of control, which is primary to development of social and emotional intelligence. In the Nurtured Heart Approach, inner wealth is developed through cumulative firsthand experiences of being held in esteem by important adults while engaging in positive behaviors or not engaging in negative behaviors. Through this aligned and enhanced energetic connection, the child comes to feel meaningful and valued.

Inner Wealth in the Classroom

What does inner wealth in the classroom look like? Teachers in classrooms where inner wealth is ingrained in the culture have less behavioral conflict; fewer children (if any) are sent out of the room; and there is an air of camaraderie and support. Teachers report that they get through lessons faster and curriculum is less disrupted. Physical education teacher BJ Byrd shares her experience of an average day with her primary-school students:

school climate

> *On this Friday in March, we were experiencing a warmer than normal day. The kids were excited to have class outdoors. We did push-up testing, which is a part of the Presidential Physical Fitness Test. I let them know that they would be able to play a few playground games while not doing the testing. I let them know that I trusted that each of them would stay on task*

and play according to the rules while enjoying this independent play time.

Fast-forward to five minutes before the end of the period. Testing was finished and I was walking toward my shed to put my equipment away. I noticed Dominick behind me. Dominick is usually quiet, focused and hard-working. On this day, he looked as though he might burst at the seams. His face had a stern look and his fists were clenched. "Dominick, are you okay?" I asked. "You look frustrated and angry."

"Brad took the ball from me and tried to hurt me," he replied, crocodile tears beginning to roll down his cheeks. I walked over and put my hand on his shoulders while bending down to his level. I said, "I am amazed at your ability to communicate so clearly what happened. I admire you for controlling your hurt and frustration. You could have retaliated against Brad, but instead, you chose to be responsible by coming over and talking with me."

Dominick looked at me while wiping away a few tears. He took a deep breath and began to relax. I saw him fully soaking up my words. Then, I turned towards the game area and noticed Brad standing about 15 feet away, quietly listening. Relentlessly, I kept talking about Dominick's greatness. "I am so proud of you for handling this in a mature, respectful manner," I said. "You were able to use your words to tell me exactly what happened and you did it in a way that Brad could hear them."

Then, I turned to Brad and said, "I see that you heard Dominick tell you how hurt and frustrated he was. In listening to him, you stood in your greatness, because it is not always easy for us to listen when we have hurt someone. Brad, I am amazed you were able to stand there so quietly."

By this time, Dominick had completely calmed down. I asked Brad, "What great thing can you do to help Dominick out?" Brad walked toward Dominick and said, "I'm sorry," while looking him in the eyes. I turned my attention back to Dominick, asking him if he felt the situation was handled, and he said, "Yes."

To both of them I said, "I want to acknowledge how both of you handled this situation. Each of you showed me what great problem solvers you are. That is a great skill to have! I' m now going to trust that both of you are going to walk back to your classroom, pick up your backpacks and head out for pick-up." With the bounce back in his step and a smile starting to appear on his face, Dominick walked back with Brad to his classroom. Both boys headed home from school knowing that they were great problem solvers.

When classrooms build inner wealth like BJ Byrd's does, children want to be there, and as a result, they are more available for learning. Attendance is higher and "teaching minutes" increase due to high levels of student engagement. In other words, according to reports from teachers across the U.S., students taught with this approach show up at a greater level; they are more prepared, despite any home pressures; and they participate more and are more motivated to learn.

BJ's students were Presidential Physical Fitness State Champions for 2009-2010 and 2010-2011 but in the second year, the number of award-winning students went from 131 to 172. The only change made in the program was the addition of the Nurtured Heart Approach.

Rhett Etherton, the author of the Foreword of this book, teaches in an inner-city school in Phoenix, Arizona. In the face of being laughed at and talked about for "trying to nurture future gang members," he held strongly to his conviction that these children deserved inner wealth as much as (if not more than) other children. He continued to purposefully, intentionally build a classroom culture of inner wealth.

The better Rhett felt about his calling, the more confident he became as a teacher and the more confident the children became. The more aware he became of his greatness, the more accessible his students were to identifying and growing their own greatness. This process can begin as soon as adults recognize the power they hold to create these experiences.

Notching it Up!

Begin to watch interactions through the lens of energy. Notice the movement of energy between people at home, at work and elsewhere. Choose a setting and spend 30 minutes observing the dynamic flow of energy.

Notice how energy is exchanged in those interactions. What does it look like when things are going well? What about when there is a problem? Share your observations below.

Think about a relationship in your life. When do you give the most energy? When do the most intense exchanges happen? What do you see happening during those exchanges when you look closely? Do you see those energetic $100 bills changing hands? Take a moment to jot down a few instances of energizing negativity.

Children's Favorite Toys

The first step to creating right-side-up energy for children is to accept that as the adult in the room, you are the center of the universe. You are the prize in any room that contains children; in fact, you're the most interesting toy they've ever seen. When it comes to buttons, lights, sounds and actions, adults have more going for them than anything on any toy store shelf. As soon as kids figure out how to get those lights, sounds and movements going—which most of them learn to do before they can talk—they're endlessly captivated. Some of those "buttons" seem to speak strongly to the intensity of certain children, especially once they perceive greater levels of response when those buttons are pushed.

In learning this approach, you'll take advantage of being such a fascinating toy by consciously modifying the ways in which you respond to the ways its buttons are pushed. Instead of inadvertently making a grand show when the "kids behaving badly" button is pushed, you'll learn to put on a (no less grand) show in response to activation of the "things are going right" button.

This concept is very much a mind-flip. It runs counter to traditional teaching paradigms. To make it work, you must believe that **your focused attention is the most important asset in that room**. Although students may sometimes seem to care not a whit about your input or approval, they are wired to do whatever's necessary to create relationship with adults. This is an intrinsic, instinctive drive.

You may be raising an eyebrow at the notion that you are this compelling.

You aren't alone; many teachers confess to feeling uncomfortable with this notion. They have the idea that academics, not the teacher, should be in the spotlight. If you agree with this, we appreciate your greatness of humility, and we ask you to question this fear. Does it come, in part, from fear of standing in your greatness? How can we expect children to stand in their greatness when we are unwilling to do the same? Greatness is what you signed up for…so own it!

> Our deepest fear is not that we are inadequate. Our deepest fear is that we are powerful beyond measure. It is our light, not our darkness that most frightens us. We ask ourselves, Who am I to be brilliant, gorgeous, talented, fabulous? Actually, who are you not to be? You are a child of God. Your playing small does not serve the world. There is nothing enlightened about shrinking so that other people won't feel insecure around you. We are all meant to shine, as children do. We were born to make manifest the glory of God that is within us. It's not just in some of us; it's in everyone. And as we let our own light shine, we unconsciously give other people permission to do the same. As we are liberated from our own fear, our presence automatically liberates others.
>
> — Marianne Williamson, *A Return to Love: Reflections on the Principles of A Course In Miracles* (Harper, 1990)

We've heard many teachers refer to students' acting out as "manipulative" or "attention-seeking." **If they mean that students are willing to do whatever it takes to get us involved in their lives in far-reaching, dynamic ways, and that they know exactly what it takes to get results, this analysis isn't far off.** But children only do this because experience has taught them that this works beautifully…and most have been learning how to work this dynamic since they were born!

If you still don't really believe that relationship with you is the greatest reward for children in your care, set an intention to behave as though you do believe this. Make an agreement with yourself to do it for one whole week, regardless of any resistance that comes up in yourself or others. Watch what transpires.

As parent or teacher, you have the power to change this upside-down flow of energy. Commit to a clear refusal to inadvertently create a pattern of the child believing that she gets more (more energy, more one-on-one time, more connection, more animation) out of meltdowns. Through that clarity, the child begins to perceive that you become his favorite toy when he is focused, acting responsibly and handling adversity well.

Dial-Up vs. Broadband

A child who's in compelling, direct relationship with an adult is connected; a child who lacks this relationship is offline. And kids don't only want connectivity. They want it fast, and they want it vivid and reliable. If you give them a choice between dial-up and broadband, which do you think they will choose? For that matter, which would you choose? Kids want broadband. Once they experience this, they don't want to go back to dial-up.

Once the child has experienced this broadband version of connection in response to efforts to extract relationship around negativity, what is the same child likely to do when a feature of a toy or game turns out to yield a sluggish, dial-up sort of connection? She might try a few different ways of approaching it, and if it still fails to yield some exciting version of connectivity, she'll abandon it. Consider that standard ways of praising and complimenting children tend to be like those uninteresting features: not responsive or energized enough to captivate a child, particularly a child who has a high level of intensity and need for energetic connection. Children tend to perceive early on that their favorite toys are just plain boring in response to good behavior. **To change this dynamic, go broadband on positivity and pull the plug on negativity**.

When Nothing's Going Wrong, Energize Success

Think about the typical classroom setting where children are working independently, and the teacher finally has time to file and record the morning homework assignments. Students are working hard, staying focused and remaining on task, and you continue to get your tasks done. Then you are summoned to one group because someone needs help. What happens next?

Inevitably, another group needs help, and the other children in the other groups become collectively restless. The high rollers begin to do their thing by upping the ante and responding to the energetic shift in the classroom, and before you know it, it's chaos.

So: what just happened? The teacher became the prize at the wrong moment. Instead of building up what was going well by actively recognizing their participation, concentration and other positive qualities, she ignored the good and focused on the bad. She became lit up when things began to fall apart.

The more intense the child, the greater his need for intense relationship, and the greater his willingness to achieve it by any means necessary. Even the most well-behaved child (or adult) has moments where his or her intensity becomes overwhelming. We all have plenty of intensity, and we can all learn to channel it toward greatness.

You're going to teach children that they get far more out of life when they live in their greatness than when they create escalating cycles of adversity. They must learn this experientially, through cumulative experiences of this energetic shift. As they see and test the change, they see that it holds up in real time. They become more attuned to right-side-up energy. They come to recognize it as the dynamic they wish to sustain. In turn, they become more tuned in to the choices and behaviors that get this energetic response. A new trajectory is forged.

Notching it Up!

Jimmy is sitting with his reading group. He has his book open to the correct page, his notebook and pencil out. He is not engaged in the discussion and looks like he might begin to annoy the people next to him any second...but so far, he hasn't.

Write three observational sentences about what is going well in this scenario. Notice both Jimmy and his group.

1. ____________________

2. ____________________

3. ____________________

Selena is fighting back giggles and distractions during the math lesson. She has her book open to the correct lesson, homework complete and ready to hand in. She looks ready to get other children to join her in distracted behavior. Write three observational sentences about what is going well in this scenario.

1. ____________________

2. ____________________

3. ____________________

Christopher is tardy again. He comes in to the classroom, hands you his tardy slip, and sits down in his seat. Write three observational sentences about what is going well in this scenario.

1. ______________________________

2. ______________________________

3. ______________________________

Danielle and Noelle come in from recess upset and bickering. They tell you about the argument they had over a boy at recess and want you to intervene. Neither has become physical and they are looking to you to solve their problem. Write three observational sentences about what is going well in this scenario.

1. ______________________________

2. ______________________________

3. ______________________________

Taking a Stand

To implement this approach, you will take three crucial Stands. We like to think of these Stands as the scaffolding from which everything else hangs. These three crucial Stands are intended to work interdependently. Without all three of them, any attempt to apply this approach will backfire.

The Stands are much like the tripod of a camera. All three legs are necessary to attain optimal balance. Removing a leg would cause the camera to topple. Each leg is as vitally important as the others, and all three must be implemented in unison. If the ground becomes unstable, the legs of the tripod must be adjusted to capture a level picture.

The Stands are:

1. **Absolutely NO:** *Refuse to energize negativity.*
2. **Absolutely YES:** *Relentlessly energize the positive.*
3. **Absolutely CLEAR:** *Establish and maintain absolute clarity around the rules, and always give an un-energized consequence when a rule is broken.*

These will all become clearer in chapters to come. For now, let's begin with the first of the three Stand of the Nurtured Heart Approach: refusal to energize negativity.

First Stand:

Absolutely NO!

I refuse to energize negativity.

Start out with a foundational refusal to give connection in response to negative behaviors. This will set the stage for more positive connectivity.

If I'm not supposed to connect to students around negativity, you might wonder, how do I give consequences for broken rules and acting out? This approach incorporates a unique take on consequences that will be described in detail in chapters to come. For now, commit simply to giving any consequence for negative behavior with as little energy and emotion as possible.

Consequences Without Negativity

Most traditional methods of doling out consequences for broken rules involve some combination of lectures, warnings, long-winded explanations about why a behavior is unacceptable, and frustrating arguments with a child over whether a rule has been broken. **All of these tactics have the same underlying problem: they create relationship around what's going wrong.**

Refusing to energize negativity does not mean looking the other way or letting them get away with unacceptable behavior. Remember: as director, producer and editor of each moment, you get to decide how you will spend your energy. You now hold an awareness of how not to spend energy when a child is being negative. By responding to negativity in an unceremonious, uncharged way, you maintain your commitment to the first Stand.

This concept is especially provocative for many teachers. We have yet to present to a group of teachers in which several standard questions do not come up: But isn't this like letting the student get away with breaking the rules or bad behavior? How will they learn the rules if I don't correct them? Isn't that my job?

These questions arise from the punitive framework typical of most traditional disciplinary methods. Looking at a classroom through this lens, you might see misbehaving children as getting away with it if the teacher doesn't respond to the child's negative behavior with an amplitude matching the degree of the transgression. Even when followed in the context of so-called positive discipline, this punitive framework will undermine your efforts. It energizes the negative and fails to energize the positive.

What would happen if you downloaded new software onto a computer that has a DOS operating system? It's fair to assume you would get all sorts of error messages; the program wouldn't run. The old operating system can't even read the new software! As a teacher, I'm calling upon you to take inventory of your internal operating system. Are you sending mixed messages about how you spend your energy in the classroom? When things get tough or you get challenged, do you default to a traditional, punitive framework?

If implemented as intended, this approach is very strict in terms of rule enforcement. **But until we flip upside-down energy right-side-up, most consequences will continue to feed students' conviction that they get more out of negativity**. Escalating consequences only feed that fire. And until students accept that they won't get energized for negative choices and that they will get the connection they crave in response to good choices, consequences won't be reliably effective.

In the chapters that follow, you'll learn how to give powerful, specific, in-the-moment, incontrovertible praise to students—tools that will enable you to give those energetic $100 bills when things are going right. As you do so, you'll set the stage for truly effective consequences. You'll see why a foundation of relentless positivity and refusal to energize negativity are essential for effective consequences.

For now, when a rule is broken, simply say, "Reset," "Time out," "Chill," or "Take a break" in the flattest, most unceremonious way possible. Or, like Rhett, create a hand signal (for example, a hand held out to say, "Stop") instead of a verbal cue. Let students know that you will no longer be lecturing them or punishing them when they break a rule, but that you'll be giving them a simple reset, after which you'll be on the lookout for their next success.

If this feels too much like jumping off a cliff for you at this point, stick with your traditional methods of giving consequences…just for now. Give those consequences with flat energy and zero emotional expressiveness.

Notching it Up!

In your own words, resolve to refuse to energize negativity. Create a "mantra" you can return to often. (If you are not familiar with this, the word mantra comes from Eastern thought and is defined as "that which protects and heals the mind.") Mantras are often used in Western psychotherapy to assist individuals in changing deeply held cognitions and perceptions. Share this mantra and its underlying intention with others if you wish to have support around this shift.

Here is an example of one of my daily mantras: "I refuse to energize negative thoughts of my own that do not support the changes I am making. I refuse to energize the negative actions of others. I will actively use the energy of any negativity I feel to become more clear about what I wish to attain."

Think about a mantra that will speak to you and support what you wish to create. Try to keep it brief; three sentences is plenty. Write it down here:

____

____

____

____

____

____

The Nurtured Heart Approach Stands and Notching It Up

The Nurtured Heart stands are the foundational tenets of the approach: three guiding principles you can fall back on any time you aren't sure how to proceed or how to correct your course when you feel you've gone in the wrong direction. Write them down and put them in a place you will see them every day. Review them often. This will help attune you when realignment is called for.

Taking a stand is about setting a firm, strong, clear intention. This is important here, because it may take a while to convince more difficult children that the old dynamic isn't operational any longer. If you allow students' resistance to derail you, the approach will never take shape in your classroom. **If you master the stands and techniques outlined here and apply them relentlessly, even the most intractable child will eventually accept the new status quo.**

A teacher I coached illustrates this point beautifully. She described a situation in which a middle school student was sent into her classroom to "regroup." This was the school protocol before sending the student to the office. Because of her advanced training in the Nurtured Heart Approach and her stellar implementation, few children acted out in her classroom. She was recognized for having a special way with even the most difficult students.

The teacher welcomed the student into the lesson and gave no energy his having been removed from his classroom, **nor did she give any hint of energy or curiosity about why the student was in trouble**. She energized the student for sitting down, although he wasn't participating in the lesson. The student continued to be disruptive in an obvious attempt to raise the stakes and challenge the teacher.

The teacher acknowledged the boy for not responding to her with aggression. In moments of calm, she recognized him for resetting. She continued to teach, acknowledge, and energize students who engaged in the lesson. Nobody gave energy to the acting-out student because the teacher was so clearly not going to give even a whiff of her own energy to the student's behavior. The student eventually gave up his quest to create chaos and even participated in the discussion.

By remaining true to this stand, the teacher was able to trust the process of the student learning the rules and culture of the classroom. She was able to follow the protocol while still implementing the approach in the purest way possible. She was relentless in her pursuit of not giving any energy to negativity and her relentlessness paid off.

Once you adopt these stands, you have an action plan when faced with a child who won't buy into right-side-up energy, but keeps trying to resurrect the old game of energy for negativity. Instead of abandoning the stands, resolve to notch them up.

Notching up the stands entails taking them to a greater level of intensity and heart-centeredness. If that level doesn't work, you take it to the next one, and the next one after that, until transformation occurs. In coming chapters of this book, you'll learn about ways to notch up your use of the approach.

Through notching up the approach, you find answers to your own questions and solve your own problems. At some point, perhaps the one at which you've notched the stands up 10 times, the approach will be effective even with the most challenging child in the room. (Most students respond to the most basic levels.)

Once you master the art of notching it up, you'll stop being afraid of difficult students. You will experience the thrill of maintaining your own personal power and influence in spite of the chaos a particular student or group of students is trying to create. Each time you maintain your integrity through these trying situations, you change the perception that you are mostly available for problems, drama, misbehavior and chaos. Notching up the approach to a place where it transforms your most difficult students ultimately benefits every child in your classroom.

Start the notching-it-up process by recognizing the truth of your inherent greatness and the inherent greatness of everyone around you. Positive values, traits, behaviors and choices are expressions of that greatness. By naming and celebrating those qualities of greatness, you open the floodgates to more of the same. Let this be the standpoint from which you begin your Nurtured Heart journey.

Chapter Three

Nurtured Heart Intentions: *Energizing the Positive*

People deal too much with the negative, with what is wrong…why not try and see positive things, to just touch those things and make them bloom?

—Thich Nhat Hanh, Buddhist monk, teacher, author and peace activist

In this chapter, we'll cover several *intentions* that will support even skeptical readers in trusting this approach. (Skepticism reflects discernment—a great quality.) These intentions support the second Stand and lay the groundwork for the techniques described in Chapters Four and Five. Together, the second and first Stands launch what we call the first phase of the Nurtured Heart Approach.

Second Stand:

Absolutely YES!

Relentlessly energize the postive.

We energize the positive by demonstrating to the child that she IS successful, *right now*. And we do so in a way that the child can't refute, no matter how hard she tries. By taking this stand, and by refusing to energize negativity, we're creating time-in: a place where inner wealth can be abundantly fed.

Resist the temptation to skip ahead to the techniques! Without the foundation of concepts that underlie the methods, the techniques are difficult to grasp and apply. We'll refer back to these intentions as we explain the techniques.

Each intention is first shared as a story or through a metaphor. Then, we'll talk about how the intention relates to the Nurtured Heart Approach, and there will be a written or experiential exercise for each intention.

See With Appreciation: The Toll Taker

One day, very early in the morning, a driver approached a toll station on the San Francisco Bay Bridge. As he scanned the booths, he saw several toll takers standing around, looking as one might expect a toll taker to look at the crack of dawn. And he saw one toll taker who appeared to be dancing.

Curious, the driver maneuvered over to the dancing toll taker's booth. As he pulled up to pay his toll, he could hear rock music blaring from a boom box inside. "Looks like you're having a fantastic time in there," he said to the toll taker.

"Sure," the toll taker replied. "What's not to love? I have the best job in the world. I get to enjoy amazing views and I have nice people to chat with all day long! Besides, I'm studying to be a dancer, and while I'm here, I get paid to practice!"

As he took his change, the driver said, "But what about all those other toll-booth attendants? They don't look like they think they have the best jobs in the world."

"Oh, those guys in the stand-up coffins?" the toll taker said. "They're no fun."[1]

We get to choose how we see our worlds. Both toll takers are in the same situation, but each is making choices about whether to be in an essentially positive or a negative place in their thoughts, emotions and actions.

The old paradigm might say that these toll takers might have had very different experiences of their lives up to the moment they showed up for work that morning. Some might have had difficult childhoods, bad breakups, or diagnoses of depression or ADHD. Others might have had great childhoods, long-lasting marriages and perfect bills of mental health. The old paradigm might maintain that these stories from the past are important dictators of the present moment. But the real truth of the moment is *the real truth of the moment!* On that day, on that morning, each person's reality was the same, and the dancing toll taker chose to embrace what was right about that reality. The other toll takers could have chosen to do the same, regardless of their life histories or relationship difficulties!

---

1. Adapted from a story by Charles Garfield, published in Jack Canfield and Mark Victor Hansen, *A 2nd Helping of Chicken Soup for the Soul* (Health Communications: Deerfield Beach, 1995), 175-177.

As director of the movie that is your life, you choose the shots, the camera angles, and all the rest of it. This is true **in this moment**, no matter what your past burdens, dramas or difficulties. Consider how empowering this is!

Notching it Up!

See this moment through the lens of the dancing toll taker. Write about your experience of this moment, focusing on what is going well and on what is not going badly that could be. Wax poetic about what you appreciate what is right and how you and those around you are successful.

'Accuse' Others of Being Successful…Right Now: *The Horse Whisperer*

In this film, Robert Redford plays the title character, Tom, who helps a young teenager, Grace, regain her confidence and love of life after an accident that caused the loss of one of her legs. In one scene, Tom teaches Grace how to drive his old pickup truck. She thinks she can't do it because of her artificial leg; but soon enough, she finds herself navigating the truck along a bumpy dirt lane. Tom tells her to keep driving until she runs out of road. "I don't think I can," she says haltingly. He replies, "It's not a question of whether you can or you can't. You are."

Tom doesn't set Grace up to achieve something in the future or reinforce her in successes past. Instead, he 'creates' her into a moment of success and calls her on it. He accuses her of being successful *right now* and gives her credit for having made it happen. He's done the groundwork to get her there, and now, all he has to do is hold up the mirror so she can see herself as irrefutably successful in this moment.

As we link specific, real-time appreciations back to the child's intrinsic greatness, we build the child's inner wealth. Negative behavior will still exist until we get to the transformative stages of this approach; however, how we address it in the moment it occurs will determine the child's perception about how to create relationship.

Direct and produce each moment from your vantage point of greatness. Address problem behaviors in an immediate, concrete and un-energized way, but in the *very first moments* you perceive the child is back on track, immediately find and express gratitude for every step the child takes in the right direction.

For example: let's say Denyse has been teasing another student. Traditional discipline approaches advise us to get down to the child's level, tell her she is breaking a rule, call a time-out, and follow up with a consequence. The consequence might entail putting her name on the board, turning her card to red, or some other version of a threat or warning. In some classrooms, teachers may also insist that she apologize.

The average child complies and is back on track within minutes. The high roller inevitably ups the ante until she is sent to the principal's office or receives some other higher level of consequence. **All of this deepens the child's existing impression that she gets more connection and relationship through adversity.**

In Nurtured Heart wisdom, the teacher purposefully intervenes as soon as she stops, even if it's just because she got distracted! You might say, "Denyse, welcome back. You've reset, and now you're being responsible and considerate." Essentially, the teacher has hijacked the child into compliance and success. She is giving the child a budding new glimpse of herself as someone who does not need problems to have connection.

Notching it Up!

Imagine you've just taught a difficult concept in an English class. One of your high-rollers was obviously confused and frustrated by the lesson. You see that instead of being disruptive, he hunkers down and tries to work through the assignment. What might you say to this child?

Try writing this same statement of appreciation in a much more specific, real-time manner. Be as precise and detailed as possible about what's going right in the exact moments that positives are happening. Keep it in the present tense.

____

____

____

Next, consider what isn't going wrong that could be. What rules aren't being broken? What negative choices aren't being made? Even if it feels silly to acknowledge poor choices not made, go ahead and try it.

____

____

____

Create Successes That Wouldn't Otherwise Exist: *Shamu's Secret*

If you've ever been to a marine park, you've probably seen an orca whale jump over a rope stretched across a pool. Have you ever tried to figure out how these massive animals are trained to do this trick? Maybe a trainer holds a fish high up in the air and waits for Shamu to jump for it, hoping he'll clear the rope strung high in the air across the water. Or maybe the rope starts out just above the water, or right on the water's surface.

Put yourself in that trainer's shoes. She's stuck in the disempowered position of having to wait for Shamu to catch on. She may have to watch and hope for a long time, vigilant for any sign that the whale might make the leap.

What the trainers actually do is start out with the rope *at the very bottom of the pool.* As soon as the whale cruises over the rope, he is rewarded with connected relationship, affection and treats. Before long, Shamu figures out how to keep the positive connection flowing, and from then on, he willingly leaps over the rope as it is raised higher.

Positive discipline advises us to "catch children being good." This Shamu intention is about doing more than that: about intentionally and relentlessly creating moments of success for children. The notion of *catching* a child doing something good implies that we might have to wait around a long, long time…especially with a highly challenging child. *Creating* these moments is about finding ways to "accuse" a child of being successful, no matter what. Shamu can't help but swim over that rope at some point when it is held at the bottom of the tank, and he gets rewarded for essentially cruising over it by accident! Once a connection is made between reward and rope, Shamu is ready to explore that potential, and the result is a spectacular leap above the water's surface.

Notching it Up!

Throughout the day, pause and notice how things are going right. Lower the rope to the very bottom of the pool. Do it to the greatest possible extreme, just as a thought experiment. Intentionally create moments of greatness in yourself and others. Write about those experiences here.

An Intention to 'Break it Down and Add it Up':
Miracles From Molecules

In the flurry of a day of teaching, most teachers hold an intention to be positive. They toss out plenty of reflections like "Good job!" and "Great work!" Sometimes they manage to slip in a more specific affirmation: "Good job staying focused!" or "Great work getting that assignment done on time." These kinds of praises are better than nothing, but they fail on two counts: 1.) They aren't specific enough, and 2.) They don't acknowledge success beyond a child's compliance with customary ideas of good classroom behavior.

The second point is important enough to repeat: ***standard modes of praise don't acknowledge successes beyond a child's compliance with customary ideas of good classroom behavior.*** In Shamu terms, they don't drop the rope to the bottom of the pool. To help him create high expectations for himself and to become intimately aware of his own gifts, great qualities and values, we reach beyond the usual superficial layer. We lower the rope.

When a child is staying focused, being quiet and sitting still, doing his work and following the rules, much more in these choices can be recognized. Most of us are good at describing what's wrong with vivid detail and plenty of animation. **What if we applied these same skills for description and observation to what's going right? *Even a child who is constantly in trouble has plenty of moments in every day when she isn't breaking any rules.*** As long as she isn't breaking any rules, you have almost infinite ways to accuse her of being successful.

Often, parents will ask for help with a particularly difficult child. When asked to describe a typical day, the adult will launch into something like this:

"She got up this morning, crabby as usual. We got into an argument over what she was going to wear to school, and then she came downstairs, ate her breakfast and got out the door on time. I didn't get any calls from school, so I assume it went well. She came home in a decent mood but pulled an attitude when it came time to do homework and get ready for bed. It turned into a meltdown, so I sent her to her room. She yelled and screamed and then came out of her room and apologized."

Not an unusual chronicle of a day in the life of an intense child, right? However: **the truth is that this child was awake for 14 hours, and in those 14 hours, she had about 20 or 30 minutes where things did not go well.** This child was successful for more than 13 hours that day!

This shift in perception is how upside-down energy gets turned right-side-up. A child who's breaking a rule is still being successful in many ways. No one can break every rule, all the time! In this approach, we need to *consciously withdraw energy when a rule is being broken,* and then *relentlessly narrate positive moments that follow.*

Picture a student, Kevin, handing in his homework on the day it's due. This might not seem like a big deal; it's what kids are supposed to do, right? Let's look at this through a new lens. *Break it down, then add it up*: look at every detail of every action until you find successes that you can reflect back to the child.

Already that day, Kevin has had to get up early enough to eat breakfast, comb his hair, get dressed, brush his teeth and wash the sleep out of his eyes. He might have had to cooperate with siblings to get access to the bathroom. He also may have made his bed, made his own breakfast and gathered his own things to put into his backpack. He's demonstrated cooperativeness, responsibility, patience and self-care…before leaving the house for school!

While doing his homework the night before, he probably demonstrated many great qualities: focus, deduction, creativity, problem-solving, and the ability to follow directions. To complete his homework last night and get it into his backpack this morning, Kevin had to be disciplined and organized. If you have any doubts about this, consider that he could have chosen not to complete his homework, or he could have left it at home. He could have filled it out illegibly or carelessly. He hasn't done any of those things: he put forth his best effort to do the assignment and to do it well.

Sit with this for a moment. Once you feel your vantage point has shifted, take a moment to consider what your "lecture" for Kevin might sound like. What would you say to this child about the *truth* of his efforts to get to school?

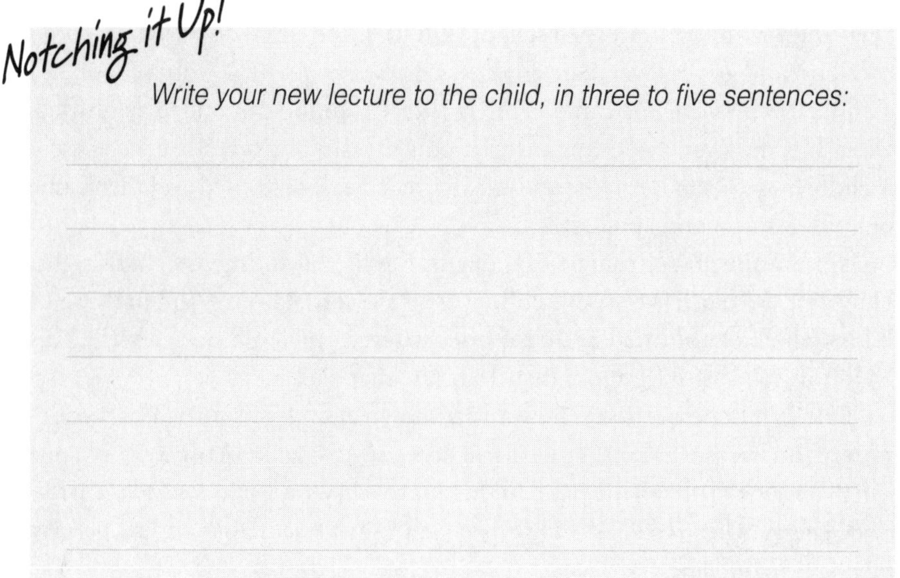

This is a challenging learning curve for nearly everyone. It takes some getting used to. Here are a few more exercises to get you started:

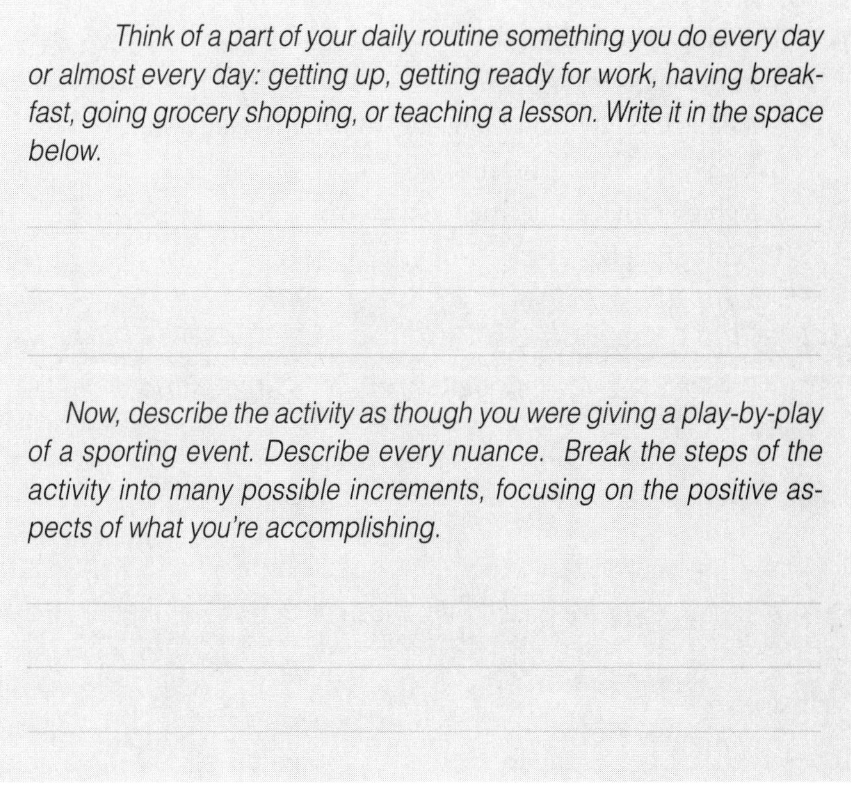

Think of a part of your daily routine something you do every day or almost every day: getting up, getting ready for work, having breakfast, going grocery shopping, or teaching a lesson. Write it in the space below.

Now, describe the activity as though you were giving a play-by-play of a sporting event. Describe every nuance. Break the steps of the activity into many possible increments, focusing on the positive aspects of what you're accomplishing.

This process of expanding upon everyday activities is a way to practice looking closer and closer at an everyday activity or choice, magnifying the pixels that make the big picture until we can see every detail of every successful choice therein.

We call this process "making miracles from molecules"—a twist on the energetically upside-down process of making mountains out of molehills. It's not a matter of whether the cup is half full or half empty; it's the greatness of whatever molecules are there for you to see. The next step is to link each of those choices to our *qualities of greatness*, which are qualities we admire in others and wish to cultivate in ourselves.

For now, consider a child who is doing nothing but sitting in his seat and staring off into the distance. One could easily feel pulled toward identifying behavior that needs correction. Yes, he might be off purpose, but for now, *look only at ways in which this child is successful.* Resist the inclination to see what is wrong; instead, focus on what is going well. What is he doing? What is he not doing? How does all of it reflect him as a successful person?

He might be:

- Thinking creative thoughts
- Taking a self-care break
- Thinking lovingly about someone who's important to him
- Taking deep, relaxing breaths
- Integrating what he's learned so far today
- Listening deeply

Notching it Up!

Add a few more examples here of what this child might be doing:

____

____

____

____

____

____

Make Time-In the Place Every Child Wants to Be: *The Video Game Time-In*

Have you noticed how video games seem to have a magically calming, focusing effect on even the most hyperactive child? They'll sit for hours, completely focused, with the solitary purpose of getting to the next level. Why are these games so compelling? We can surmise that it's their entertainment value, but the fact is that the *structure* of these games is what makes them so appealing.

Video games provide a perfect blend of consequences and acknowledgement. The rules of the game are clear and consistent, and so are the incentives. As soon as you break a rule, you are notified and a consequence is given. Immediately, though, you reset and begin again. The game doesn't remind you about the last mistake or lecture you about your poor choices. It simply starts over.

Do children learn the rules of video games by reading the manual? NEVER! They learn by breaking the rules, receiving an immediate and clear consequence, and beginning again with a clean slate. The game does not change based on what kind of day it had, whether it's in a good mood, or whether it's having relationship problems. The game is the game…is the game!

To the intense child, having a defined structure of predictable consequences and rewards strongly defines the lines within which she can stay in time-in. Having those strongly defined lines feels good. It feels secure.

As long as the child stays in the video game, time-in is created through sounds, visual images and the accrual of points. Children can count on this time-in as long as they are not breaking rules, answering questions incorrectly or making other game-ending errors. When they do make a mistake, they might be out of the game, but all they need to do to get back to success is *reset* and start over. Although a video game consequence might involve virtual dismemberment or something similarly gory, it is fundamentally an illusion. The child is back in the game in a matter of seconds. It's just a way to start over.

Video games, whether innocuous math or spelling games or violent, blow-'em-up games, *reliably energize success and fail to energize rule-breaking or mistakes.* Through the techniques introduced in the next two chapters, you'll learn how to reliably reproduce this right-side-up energy in your classroom. You might find that the same techniques work in other areas of your life too.

Notching it Up!

As you move through your day, apply the concept of the video game time-in to your interactions. Emulate the video game in the way you refuse to energize negativity and pour your energy into reinforcement of every increment of good choices. Journal here about your observations and experiences.

Phase I Complete!

You've reached a true launching-off point: a deep understanding of the first two stands and the intentions that drive them forward. This is what we call Phase I, and with it, you possess the groundwork for mastery of the techniques laid out in the next two chapters.

As you move on, keep in mind that **superficial praise or energizing in a way that is sarcastic or insincere will only breed distrust and rebellion.** As you begin to use the techniques described in the next two chapters, focus on authenticity: on being truly in your heart.

Notch It Up...to Greatness

This transformation requires a shift from the traditional good vs. bad dichotomy. According to the good vs. bad paradigm, if students are being good, there s always the possibility that things will go south and the fear that this could happen. This fear tends to create exactly what we are trying to avoid.

Begin to notch it up by seeing anything that goes wrong or could go wrong as an energy that you can play with. As the 13th century poet Rumi said: "Out beyond ideas of rightdoing and wrongdoing, there is a field. I'll meet you there." That field is greatness.

Chapter Four

Techniques For Creating Time-In, Part I: *Active and Experiential Recognitions*

People are just about as happy as they make their minds up to be.

—Abraham Lincoln

In choosing to adopt this approach, you're making your mind up to be happy. The techniques you'll learn and practice in this chapter and the following chapter are tools for seeing the world less like the guys in the stand-up coffins and more like the dancing toll taker. Prepare to go beyond the dichotomy of whether the cup is half-full or half-empty to choosing to view the beauty of whatever is there.

The techniques of the Nurtured Heart Approach are designed to activate the three Stands. In particular, the four techniques described in this chapter and the one following put wind beneath the wings of the second Stand (energizing success). You'll see that these methods also make adherence to the first Stand (refusing to energize negativity) much easier.

Nurtured Heart Approach techniques are intended to help you convey honest, heart-centered feedback about *ordinary actions, moments and emotions.* They equip you to do so in a way that will give you the power to *create moments where children are **being** great* (instead of merely trying to "catch them being good") *in their normal modes of activity.* You don't have to wait around for anything spectacular. Instead, show them that they are seen and acknowledged just for meeting everyday expectations. Refusing to energize negativity and applying these techniques flips upside-down energy right-side up.

These techniques give specific tools for perceiving and verbally acknowledging every facet of positive choices and attitudes. The aim here is to create the broadest possible range of ways to appreciate a child in a moment where he is successful (which includes any moment when he is not breaking a rule). Purposefully and intentionally create success at every turn. *Any choice to follow a rule, any rule, is a choice that can be celebrated.* Each time we choose to recognize a positive choice, we add to the child's inner wealth.

As you learn to give these acknowledgements, you create a vibrant time-in, where students feel an energetic connection around what's going right...*and* around what's not going wrong. By creating a juicy time-in, you convey an underlying message: "Yes, you are doing the right thing, not the wrong thing; and yes, you are highly valued and meaningful...here's the proof." It conveys, "I value *you* for who *you* are, and you can have confidence in your own value, too."

We're not fans of formulas or cookie-cutter ways of implementing, because we believe that energizing must come from the heart. Still, we realize that some people do better with a more formulaic way to begin implementing the approach. If this describes you, we recommend a formula for successful time-in called the **80/20 rule: 80 percent or more of interactions in time-in and 20 percent or fewer in resets.** If you aspire to adhere to this formula, you will be well on your way to successful implementation. If you stay with the absolute truth of the moment, and if you commit to seeing every nuance of what's going right in each of those moments, this criterion is an easy one to meet.

This 80/20 rule may be reminiscent of rules of other approaches regarding ratios of praise to criticism. The Nurtured Heart Approach does not advocate criticism and does not stop at traditional praise. Within the context of Nurtured Heart, time-out is not a criticism of a child's choice; nor is it a negative place to be. It is a simple pause in the action; there is no judgement, just a reset back to greatness.

Learning a New Language...

If you have ever been to a foreign country, you know that there is always a period of adjustment. You have to decipher the customs and language in order to get your needs met. In your first few hours, you are most focused on figuring out where you will sleep, how you'll get there, and what you'll eat. As time goes on, you come to feel more secure in getting your basic needs met and can tune in more to expressing yourself and learning the language. When you first try to speak in that foreign tongue, you feel awkward, maybe even clumsy. But as time goes on, you become more comfortable and confident in your ability to communicate.

When learning a new language, you begin with grammar, sentence structure and vocabulary, but at a certain point, all those memorized conjugations and rules and definitions fly out the window as you express yourself fluently. The same will happen with the Nurtured Heart techniques. They will stop feeling like techniques as you become fluent in this language for relating in positivity.

Four essential techniques make up the Nurtured Heart toolbox. Each technique builds on the one that precedes it, and eventually, you'll become better able to combine the techniques on the fly. Although presented individually, they are intended to work interdependently, much as grammatical rules work interdependently within a single sentence. This is a new language you're learning; be patient with yourself. In waiting this long to get to techniques for propelling positivity and radical appreciation, you've already demonstrated great patience!

...and Cultivating a Self-Forgiving Attitude

When you feel yourself falling into negativity or falling short of your own expectations, you'll want to have these Stands in mind. *Reset to the Stands and use any energy of frustration to propel greater determination from this moment forward.* Pause, take a breath into your heart, say your mantras out loud, and begin again as though this were the first moment in time (because, ultimately, all we have is this moment).

The four techniques for energizing and recognizing success are:

1. **Active Recognition**
2. **Proactive Recognition**
3. **Experiential Recognition**
4. **Creative Recognition**

The four Nurtured Heart techniques for energizing and recognizing success will enable you to irrefutably point out a current expression of greatness at any time! In doing so, you are stepping into your power in a whole new way.

General Pointers for Nurtured Heart Recognitions In The Classroom

✓ *Give recognitions loud and clear so that the whole room can hear them.* One-on-one recognitions may sometimes feel appropriate, but generally, recognitions that are audible to all students will benefit the whole classroom. (Take care, though, not to give recognitions in a way that shames or humiliates those in the room who are not recipients of the current recognition.)

✓ *Adopt a tone and style that honestly reflects you as an individual.* Some adults are comfortable with a more energetic, openly enthusiastic delivery, because that's how they like to communicate. Others are equally effective with a more low-key delivery. Convey your recognitions in a way that feels honest and that comes from your heart.

✓ *Never give recognitions to students who are in the act of breaking rules.* Rule-breaking is met with an un-energized "Reset!"—which will be described in detail in Chapter Six. Giving a recognition to a child who isn't pushing boundaries will impact children who are. When they see your energy going towards a child who is not acting out, they'll eventually get that their favorite toy is responding differently than it once did—and that negative behaviors won't get them into this new game.

✓ Remember the first two Stands. If you get flustered or confused about what to do next, repeat the stands in your head or aloud before proceeding.

✓ Avoid warnings or dangling carrots. Warnings, although well intentioned, convey fear and energize negativity. Offering a reward for something you want a child to do will cause high-rollers to further attempt to extract energy for negativity with a refusal.

✓ *When you encounter resistance, notch it up!* Try to see the resistance as energy waiting to be channeled in a different direction. *Commit to remaining positive as though your life depended on it.*

Technique #1: *Active Recognition*

Take a verbal "snapshot" of an everyday moment. Describe what you see as though you were describing it to a person who is visually impaired.

Using neutral, non-judgemental, specific language, report to the child what you see, hear and sense when you observe him or her. Include observations of activities and emotional states. Use the child's name somewhere in the recognition. Think of these as "Kodak moments," which helps convey the photographic, non-interpretive quality of this kind of recognition.

"Christopher, I see that you are setting up your materials for the next lesson."

"Danielle, I see you're making a collage with purple, red and yellow tissue paper. You're using the paste brush to glue them in a pattern that looks like a flower." (Note that this is very different than saying, " Danielle, I like your picture. You are a good artist.")

"Dave, I hear you telling Amber about your trip to see your grandparents. I see that Amber is listening intently to your story." (Very different from, "You're doing a good job talking about the trip.")

An Active Recognition entails holding up a mirror to the child in moments when **nothing is going wrong**. Tell **the absolute truth of the moment**—just the facts, without telling any stories about those facts or defaulting to the past or the future.

Notching it Up!

Create a few of your own sample Active Recognitions/Kodak moments based on observation of students, family members or colleagues. Use as much detail as possible. Avoid any kind of value judgment. For example, if Sarah is painting a picture, you might say, "Sarah, I see you are using the brush and your eyes are focused on the paper." Heres a few to get you started:

Rachel, I see you filling in your agenda.

Zooey, I see you sitting with your group while at the same time having your eyes focused on me.

James, you are passing out the snack to all of your classmates.

Is Too Much Praise Bad For Children?

In recent years, several studies on the value of praising children made the news with headlines like, "Are Kids Getting Too Much Praise?" (*New York Times*, October 29, 2007) and "Are We Raising a Nation of Little Egomaniacs?" (msnbc.msn.com, April 2, 2007).

In one study performed at Stanford University, scientists divided a group of children in half and gave each group the same test. When they finished, one group was told they did well because they were *smart* or *intelligent* while the other group was told they did well because they tried hard. When both groups were given a chance to take the test again to potentially get a better score, 90 percent of the latter group wanted to try again, while most of those in the first group were reluctant. And when the second round of tests was completed, the group that was told it was smarter did considerably worse.[1]

The problem isn't *too much* praise; it's the *wrong kind* of praise. Cheerleading ("Good job! Way to go! You're smart! You're awesome!") does not serve the child. It might give a temporary lift, but in the end, the child doesn't believe it. *He wants to know:* ***How*** *am I good?* ***What*** *exactly did I do right? What did I do that was smart; what choice did I make that was awesome?* Children are wired to seek this kind of specificity. It's through this that they learn, in an experiential way, how to move through their worlds and relate to others.

Giving bold, effective praise is a specific and reverent process. It involves calling out aspects of the child's behaviors and personality *as they are expressed in the moment.* This immediacy and specificity takes positive statements of appreciation, recognition and acknowledgment to a transformative level.

What Is the Point of Active Recognition?

Although this method won't initially sound like positivity or appreciation—after all, there's no value judgement, no variations on "good job!" or "wow, what an accomplishment!"—*it is perceived as a positive recognition by the child.*

When a child receives an acknowledgement like this, he feels seen, heard and appreciated for everyday contribution. Active Recognition provides a pathway for us to shift the child's perception that he gets more through negativity. As children shift, they begin to anticipate the benefits of the new pattern.

If children simply stop negative behavior and have no other way to get us involved and connected, they have no motivation to stay in their new pattern. Intense children need assurance that they don't become invisible when they are acting appropriately. Active Recognition demonstrates to children that they

1. Mueller CM, Dweck CS, "Praise for Intelligence Can Undermine Children's Motivation and Performance," *Journal of Personality and Social Psychology,* 1998, Vol 75, No. 1, 33-52.

are seen, heard and related to with energy when they are *not* acting out. They see that they don't have to hit the high watermarks of success to be appreciated.

Active Recognition harmonizes with the intentions of the approach: To create successes that would not otherwise exist (Shamu), to choose to see successes (Toll Taker) and to create miracles from molecules by vastly expanding the ways we can make a child feel honored. It's a technique that helps us catch every opportunity to connect with children in a positive manner.

Notching it Up!

Set a timer for five minutes and sit down with your child or other family members. Actively recognize as many times as you can and keep track of the number of recognitions with hashmarks. At the end of the five minutes, observe the child. Do you see behavioral changes, changes in mood or other changes? Also notice what's going on for you. Do you feel tired? Energized?

Jot down some of your recognitions and anything else you want to remember about the impact of this initial experience of the approach below.

Begin to weave Active Recognitions into your day. Give them abundantly to your students, your colleagues, and to yourself. Notice how simply being acknowledged inspires students to seek out more success.

Take a day or a few days before moving on to the next technique; give at least 10 Active Recognitions each day in your classroom (and anywhere else you see fit). Work up to 10 Active Recognitions each hour. Keep track for yourself until it becomes second nature.

Technique #2: Experiential Recognition

Say what you see and attach value.

The next technique, Experiential Recognition, builds on Active Recognition. It entails verbal acknowledgement of desirable *values* and *qualities of greatness* as they are expressed in the child's everyday actions.

Notching it Up!

Think back to the last time you discussed values with a child especially a challenging child. What were the surrounding circumstances? What did you say? How did the child respond?

Most likely, your last conversation about values with a child was in response to an episode where the child did *not* express or uphold the value in question.

We lecture about responsibility when a child doesn't turn in homework; we lecture about generosity when a child won't share; we lecture about honesty when a child is caught in a lie; or we lecture about nonviolence in the aftermath of a shove, a hit or bullying. We treat ourselves the same way, dressing ourselves down for failing to uphold values that are important to us.

We all know these lectures don't work on others or on ourselves. The average human being does not respond well to being exhorted to do better in the aftermath of a vividly described failure! In the worst case, a child who is invested in getting energized connection by any means necessary will deepen his refusal to live positive values because he gets a lot more adult focus and acknowledgement when he doesn't. He doesn't do this on purpose; he wants energetic connection and knows where to get more, faster. It's dial-up vs. broadband. Broadband always wins.

With Experiential Recognitions (also known as "Polaroid moments") we talk about desirable values *only when they are being exhibited by the child.* Each time we do this, the child has an in-the-moment experience of *living desirable values and qualities.* With each of these experiences, the child's image of him or herself as someone who is successful and good grows and expands. Inner wealth is amplified and magnified.

What Are Values?

Values are *beliefs of a person or social group in which they have an emotional investment.* As a culture, we are invested in responsibility, honesty, generosity, and nonviolence; these are examples of values when we look at them as norms or part of a belief system imposed on individuals by their culture.

We can also look at these values as *expressions of each person's intrinsic greatness.* Rather than seeing values as behaviors *others* want to see from *us*—behaviors that we engage in because of others' expectations—we can choose to see them as qualities intrinsic to who we are. Through this lens, we can see values as *expressions of the greatness that exists within each of us.* Values and qualities of greatness are interchangeable.

Try this activity to get more comfortable with the language of the approach. Choose five words from the list below that really resonate with you. Write them on Post-it notes and place them in areas where you will see them daily: your bathroom mirror, for example, or the door of your refrigerator or the dashboard of your car. *Wear these words out* in your vocabulary by actively recognizing yourself, your students, your coworkers, even strangers, using these words as often as possible. Do this until they become second nature. Then, choose five more.

List of Values/Qualities of Greatness

Abundance – Acceptance – Accuracy – Activism – Adaptability – Adventurousness – Affection – Agility – Alertness – Altruism – Articulateness – Assertiveness – Attentiveness – Awareness – Audacity – Balance – Benevolence – Boldness – Candor – Clarity – Cleverness – Collaboration – Compassion – Confidence – Connection – Conscientious – Caring – Consideration – Cooperation – Courage – Courtesy – Curiosity – Daring – Dedication – Depth – Determination – Dignity – Discernment – Differentiation – Discretion – Efficiency – Elation – Elegance – Empathy – Endurance – Energy – Expansiveness – Experimentation – Fairness – Faith – Fearless – Ferocity – Fidelity – Flexibility – Flow – Focus – Forethought – Forgiveness – Friendship – Frugality – Fun – Generosity – Good judgment – Good manners – Good

Sportsmanship – Gratitude – Guidance – Harmony – Healing – Heart – Helpful – Honesty – Hope – Humility – Humor – Imagination – Independence – Industry – Inquisitiveness – Intelligence – Insight – Integrity – Intensity – Intuition – Joy – Justice/Being Just – Kindness – Knowledge – Laughter – Leadership – Loving – Loyalty – Mastery – Mindfulness – Observation - Open-mindedness – Openness – Organization – Originality – Passion – Patience – Peaceful – Perceptive – Perseverance – Perspective – Playfulness – Power – Precision – Productiveness – Professionalism – Reason – Receiving – Relaxation – Resilience – Resolve – Respect – Responsibility – Restraint – Reverence – Sacrifice – Security – Self-control – Self-mastery – Sensitivity – Service – Spirituality – Spontaneity – Spunk – Stability – Stealth – Stillness – Strength – Sympathy – Synergy – Teamwork – Thoroughness – Thoughtfulness – Thrift – Tolerance – Tranquility – Unflappability – Unity – Uniqueness – Valor – Vibrancy – Vigor – Virtue – Vision – Warmth - Warriorship (positive power) – Willingness – Wisdom – Wit – Zeal

Add any other qualities of greatness you wish to recognize in the space provided below:

____

____

____

One way to give an Experiential Recognition is to start with an Active Recognition as a way of framing the truth of the moment, then finding a quality of greatness that is being lived by the child in that moment and pointing it out. **A sentence structure for this might be: (Child's name), I see you _______________ (Active Recognition); that tells me you are/have the quality of _______________ (Experiential Recognition).**

"Melissa, I see you lending Charlie a pencil. You're being generous and thoughtful."

"Howie, you're drawing purple cars and green planes for your art project. I see you've even put tiny people inside. What a creative spin and attention to detail!"

(For a very young child:) "Alice, you're trying to sharpen your pencil on your own rather than asking me for help. You're showing me that you are self-sufficient and independent...that you like doing things on your own."

(For a teenager:) "Amy, you're staying quiet and focused in the middle of lots of talking and activity. Great example you're setting. You're being tolerant and productive."

You can always add a comment about how the qualities being pointed out are reflections of the ground truth of the greatness that every child possesses.

For example:

- After recognizing Howie for his drawing, you could add: "Attention to detail and creativity are both qualities of your greatness."
- After recognizing Alice, add: "Self-sufficiency and independence are part of your greatness."

Break down what you see into its smallest component parts to actively seek moments where the child can be "accused" of living out his or her greatness. Howard calls this *pixelation.* You're zooming in to the picture of the child's actions as far as necessary to find greatness. You are doing much more than catching the child being good; *you are creating the child being great*—reminding the child that greatness is always present and awaiting expression.

It is our job to make their intrinsic greatness tangible and concrete through calling them out on their greatness. In doing so, we make *miracles from molecules!*

Experiential Recognition is a wonderful tool for introducing new words that describe values, great qualities and emotions. What better way for a child to grasp the meaning of words like these than to be shown how they are already living or expressing them? Remember the Horse Whisperer, who irrefutably demonstrated to Grace that she *could* drive the truck...that, in fact, she already was.

Notching it Up!

Below are a few Active Recognitions. Below each one, jot in qualities of greatness/positive values that relate to the child's choice. Feel free to use the lists on pages 67-68 and 72-73. Then, choose one of those qualities/values and create an Experiential Recognition.

"Noelle, you're working steadily on your project, even though there's a lot of noise and commotion going on around you."

Qualities of greatness:

Experiential recognition for Noelle:

"Nathaniel, I see you searching around in your backpack for something."

Qualities of greatness:

Experiential recognition for Nathaniel:

"Tristen, I hear you getting frustrated with the assignment. You've pushed yourself back from your desk to take a break."

Qualities of greatness:

Experiential recognition for Tristen:

"CJ, you're sitting at your desk, so still and quiet, looking straight ahead...but you're tapping one foot really fast."

Qualities of greatness:

Experiential recognition for CJ:

As you begin to experiment with Experiential Recognition in your classroom, jot down a few of your own here. How have your students responded?

To our readers: We applaud your great determination and intention in getting this second stand of positivity going while still holding fast to the first stand of refusing to energize negativity. Phase I of the Nurtured Heart Approach is well underway.

For all children, both Active Recognitions and Experiential Recognitions of emotional states are especially powerful. When we observe and comment on a child's emotions—especially when they're strong emotions, or emotions that are generally considered negative, such as anger, frustration, sadness or fear—we demonstrate that any feeling is okay to have. Remember, even a child who is angry is (more often than not) handling anger in a healthy way. She's not screaming. She uses words to express herself, or she takes a moment by herself to regroup.

Parents and teachers often have a difficult time allowing children to feel uncomfortable emotions. We avoid allowing them to be sad or frustrated, but this is exactly where we lose ground in teaching our children how to be emotionally competent. When children learn to be uncomfortable, frustrated and sad in healthy ways, and when they are reinforced for handling themselves well when things are hard, they learn to cope. They stop living in fear of uncomfortable feelings.

"Nicholas, I see that you're feeling angry right now, but you're choosing to keep your cool."

"Sophia, you're very sad. You're having big feelings right now and you are using words to express them. That's showing courage and trust to know you can say what you are feeling in a way others can hear."

"Michael, you're really frustrated right now and you are keeping you're hands to yourself. That's hard to do when you are upset. That takes a lot of healthy power!"

"Mary Jo, I see you're disappointed that you don't have cookies in your lunch, like Manny does...it looks like you're feeling envious and you're handling that strong feeling so well by not making a fuss and eating your lunch without complaining."

By non-judgmentally holding up the mirror to a child who is successfully dealing with strong emotions (meaning, without breaking rules), we help the child to dissociate the acting-out of difficult emotions from the simple experience of feeling them.

Feelings/Emotional States to Recognize

(Feelings/emotions printed in bold type are the most common emotions and the easiest to remember to recognize.)

Acceptance – Agitation – Alarm – Amusement – ***Anger*** *– Angst – Annoyance – Anticipation – Anxiety – Apprehension – Aversion – Awe – Bitterness – Boredom – Bewilderment – Betrayal – Calm – Cautiousness – Closeness – Comfort – Compassion – Contentedness – Confidence – Confusion – Courage – Disappointment – Discontent – Disgust – Delight – Determination – Distress - Doubt – Emptiness – Elation – Euphoria – Embarrassment – Empathy – Enjoyment – Enthusiasm – Envy – Ecstasy –* ***Fear*** *– Frustration – Gladness – Gratitude – Greed – Grief – Guilt – Happiness – Homesickness – Honor – Hope – Horror – Humility – Hurt – Impatience – Indignation – Interest – Irritation – Isolation –* ***Joy*** *– Jealousy – Loneliness –* ***Love*** *– Modesty – Misunderstood – Rejection – Nervousness – Nostalgia – Panic – Patience – Peacefulness – Pride – Rage – Regret – Remorse – Resentfulness –* ***Sadness*** *– Satisfaction – Shame – Shyness – Shock*

– Suffering – Surprise – Suspense – Sympathy – Terror – Tiredness – Troubled – Trust – Understanding – Vulnerability – Wonder – Worry – Yearning – Zest

When a challenging emotion is acknowledged and allowed, and when it isn't acted upon in a way that leads to rule-breaking, success is happening. Active and Experiential Recognitions are highly effective with children who are emotionally wound up or who are highly invested in the old status quo of energy for negativity.

Notching it Up!

Take a moment to turn the phrases below into Active and/or Experiential Recognitions. If you feel stuck, try using a general sentence structure like this one, but don't worry about sticking with it in any strict way:

_______________ (Name), I see you _______________ (Behavior),

and what that says about you is _______________ (Value).

1. Crying over spilled milk

Example: "Howie, I see you are upset that your milk spilled, but you're cleaning it up without fussing. That tells me that you are responsible and mature."

Or: "Howie, I see you've spilled your milk, and I see you crying. What that says about you is that you prefer not to waste food. You appreciate what you have. And you don't want to make extra work for the custodian. That shows me you're considerate and grateful for what you have."

2. Angry about losing a game

Example: "Melissa, I see that losing the game is frustrating for you. Even though you lost, you're willing to start over and keep trying. That tells me that you have perseverance."

3. Being embarrassed about falling down at recess

4. Upset about being picked on

5. Frustrated and anxious over failing a test

6. Being bullied

7. In an argument with a friend

8. Being sent to the principal's office

"Do Something Great…or Be Greatness in a Way That is You."

When finding your way to an Experiential Recognition (or to any recognition at all!) feels difficult, try simply remarking on a quality that is intrinsic to the child. Maybe she's naturally quiet, or energetic, or outgoing, or generous, or good at communicating. Even when the child is doing absolutely nothing, you can find ways to recognize the greatness she brings not through what she does or says, but just through the quality and power of her presence in the room. In doing so, you call the child out for just being the greatness that she is.

"Noah, you have such natural joy. Your presence always brings extra fun to the room!"

"Sherry, your calmness is so soothing. You have a serenity that helps all of us stay focused."

"Drew, I so appreciate your inquisitive nature. You ask questions and probe to find answers. That just seems to be the way you're wired, and it always helps the rest of us learn more!"

Notching it Up!

Think about students you would most like to support in shifting to positive choices. Write down a few of their intrinsic positive qualities. Make a point of remarking upon those qualities in the classroom in the context of Experiential Recognitions.

Energizing Students Creates More Energy In Educators

Teachers are some of the most multi-faceted people we know. They are educators, parents, gardeners, janitors, computer experts, electricians, comedians, janitors, healers, marathoners, magicians and therapists all rolled into one. As an observer of so many teachers, we've come to think of them much like those circus performers who spin plates on sticks. If those plates aren't kept spinning constantly, they come crashing down one by one.

If all this talk of having you create this intense time-in for students has you exhausted at the starting gate, consider this: intense children will consume energy in any form. They will get us, their favorite toys, to light up—if not for the good stuff, then for the bad. It's up to us to make our energy available when a child is making choices we wish to reinforce.

Teachers who dedicate themselves to these stands in the classroom report that they rarely have discipline problems. As children are imbued with inner wealth, they become more invested in being part of the positive culture of their classroom despite any difficulties they face at home.

The more energy you spend on success, the more successful everyone will feel. In the end, you will find that these efforts are the *opposite* of draining. One teacher I recently spoke with described this as "a different kind of tired." She said that instead of coming home emotionally exhausted and needing a glass of wine, she now comes home emotionally full but physically tired. She likened this to injuring a muscle versus the soreness that comes from building a muscle through yoga or weightlifting. With the latter, it's a good kind of *sore*—the kind that promotes growth.

Notching it Up!

Imagine you have just read this chapter of the workbook, and you're excited to try to implement some of the techniques and new language of the approach. You're met with resistance, nervousness and outright disrespect. Your challenge is to address these dynamics in keeping with the first two stands:

1. ***Absolutely No! Refusal to energize negativity; and***
2. ***Absolutely Yes! Relentlessly energize the positive.***

Take a moment to write down what you might say to address these students.

Remembering the First Stand

By now, you have certainly encountered some level of resistance. Keep remembering your first stand: to *refuse to energize negativity.* Simply refuse to give it your time, your energy, or any aspect of your being.

When negativity emerges, you have two options in the context of the approach:

1. If no rules are being broken, look for something that is going right, ei-

ther with the child who is expressing the emerging negativity or with another child in the room, and verbally acknowledge it using one of the first two techniques.

2. If a rule is being broken, say the child's name and "Reset," without any warnings or strong emotional expression. Once the rule-breaking stops, immediately give an Active or Experiential Recognition that includes feedback on how well the child reset herself back into success and greatness. (Remember: the reset will be covered in much more depth in Chapter Six.)

If negativity emerges for you, as it inevitably will, combine these two options: give yourself a reset (2) and then look for something that's going right in yourself or in the classroom (1). Do it out loud if you like; students love to see teachers resetting themselves. Everyone will leak negativity at times, and everyone has the power to reset themselves away from it when it comes up.

It may sound something like, "I need the class to take a reset with me right now." Take a few deep breaths. "Okay, I'm ready to go. All of you showed great integrity in resetting with me. Let's move on!"

Tips for Summoning Up Authentic Recognitions

When it feels difficult or impossible to summon up a single heartfelt appreciation or recognition, consider:

- ✓ We all know what it's like to deal with a child who is unwilling to follow the rules. Depending on our level of composure, we might feel frustration, anger, or fear when faced with a student who is determined to upend the room. **Let this fuel *real gratitude* about students who *are* following the rules; let that gratitude fuel your recognitions.** "I want to energize table two right now. There is a lot going on, and you continue to stay focused and work through the math problems. Great teamwork!"
- ✓ When you do become frustrated, angry or fearful, **let those emotions surge through you**…and then, **channel them into your own greatness, letting that emerge in your next round of recognitions.** Be willing to acknowledge yourself either silently or verbally for hanging in there, not leaking, resetting yourself, taking a stand, and not feeding negativity.

✓ Be willing to flip upside-down energy right-side-up as soon as you feel yourself going down the road toward negative lectures or pointless discussions about misdeeds and mistakes. **Go ahead and lecture your students, but only about things that are going right. Have long discussions about successes instead of failures.** Make a fuss or be confrontational, but only about all you are appreciating: a much better, much more beneficial way of making a big deal. "Class, I want to acknowledge everyone who has their eyes on their work. If you have already started your work you are demonstrating great leadership right now. By working hard right now, you are also being collaborative and cooperative. Those are all qualities of your greatness. Raise your hand if this describes who you are in this moment. Again, being engaged is what great learners do! You are all demonstrating what it is to be a great leader."

The next two techniques for giving energized recognitions are covered in the next chapter. ***Give yourself some time to integrate these first two techniques into your days in the classroom before moving on.***

Notching it Up!

Create your own mantra around the first two stands. How does energizing the positive affect your heart? Your daily choices? Your overall outlook? A personal mantra might be: "I am a powerful and wise teacher. As I reflect the greatness of others, I honor my own wisdom."

In this context, a mantra serves the purpose of keeping your intention and purpose front and center in your mind. If you repeat it often, you are more likely to make it a part of your belief system. By having a mantra, you will have a reminder at the moment when "the rubber meets the road" and you are most likely to go back to past teaching paradigms.

Your "mantra" for the first stand:

Your "mantra" for the second stand:

Chapter Five

Techniques For Creating Time-In, Part II: *Proactive and Creative Recognitions*

Consciousness is transmitted in relationships. We seek friends, lovers, communities, who can see us, hold us, bear us...Likewise, we construct our circle of friends and our communities and then they construct us precisely by how they see us into being...For the real self to emerge, we urgently need a social network of appropriate self-objects who love, support, challenge, and sustain us.

—Psychotherapist and yoga teacher Stephen Cope[1]

Schoolday mornings are often cited as the most difficult times by parents of challenging children. Every day, these children will refuse to get out of bed and seem to forget their morning routines. Getting a difficult child to school on time without frustration, lectures, warnings, or threatened consequences can come to seem impossible.

But what if that child's mother gave him 100 points just for opening his eyes in the morning? What if she gave him another 100 points for getting out of bed, and an additional 100 points for getting dressed? Imagine the kind of day this child would have after being held in esteem for the most basic positive choices. And imagine the joy everyone would experience with this new morning ritual.

In this context, the points don't mean anything besides *giving the child the perception that he is winning.* Recognitions give the child energetic "points" for every increment of success. This is the video game time-in, which inspires even the most difficult child to perform the best she can in this new game of greatness: to climb level after level to new heights of mastery and accomplishment.

Stop, take a breath, and let yourself feel the truth of this. Before you move ahead into the next technique, see the greatness of your own willingness to make this shift.

We are, in large part, created by the way others mirror us. This is never truer in our lives than during childhood. By learning ways in which to mirror the children in our lives when they are doing things right, we provide them with an irrefutable picture of their greatness—their true nature. We polish that mir-

---

1. *Yoga and the Quest for the True Self,* Bantam Books, 2000; page166.

ror, creating brilliant clarity around the truth of even the smallest successes.

The next technique expands upon your ability to reflect and reinforce greatness through rules. For most readers, this will involve a tweaking of current rules, and (probably) the addition of at least a few new rules. You'll find that with this approach, the more rules you have in place, the more inspiration you'll have to acknowledge greatness in all the small ways it shows up. When students start to see this, they will welcome every new rule you create for your classroom.

'Shamu-ing' To Success

With Proactive Recognition, we demonstrate our willingness to move the figurative rope of success as low as necessary, even to the bottom of the pool. The goal is to make success absolutely inevitable.

With children who don't often break rules, Proactive Recognitions will deepen the way in which the rules resonate for them. Those "good" children will see how rules work in their favor to keep their worlds organized. They'll see that success and appreciation are always within the bounds of their worlds.

Proactive Recognitions give the educator the power to capture and reflect moments of success, even with the most resistant, difficult students. No one can break all rules all the time, and so we can always find a way to create moments of success for a student in any moment when rules are not being broken.

Technique #3: *Proactive Recognition*

Accuse the child of NOT breaking the rules.

Just as most of us default into lecturing children about values when they are not embodying them, **we tend to talk about rules when they are not being followed.** We wax poetic about the rules when they are broken and give highly energized warnings to students who seem poised to cross the line.

How many of us believe we are being proactive by being *extra firm* in those moments or by reminding children of an impending consequence for breaking the rules? The problem with this is that intense children are attuned to every incremental shift in the energy of interactions with adults. They smell fear like a shark smells blood! Students who want to create energized relationship with educators often can do so simply by moving toward the line between rule followed and rule broken. This traditional disciplinary approach to rules plays right into upside-down energy.

It is important to remember that this is not a calculated decision on the child's part. It is based on repeated experiences with adults where they see, in living color and surround-sound, exactly how to get *more* out of the adults in their lives: more energy, more intensity, more quality and quantity of time and relationship.

On some days, we might react with consequences, lectures or warnings when a student appears to be moving toward rule-breaking or even just *thinking* about moving toward it. Some kids are highly skilled at making the lights, sounds and actions of their favorite toys pop without even touching a button. Kids labeled as troublemakers often get big doses of adult energy in response to adults' expectations that they're more likely to break rules than other kids. By now, you see how this perpetuates the $100-bucks-for-broken-rules dynamic.

Proactive Recognitions (also known as Canon moments) are about *energizing children for failing to break the rules.* Students learn about the rules and the benefits of following them, but this happens when they ARE following the rules, not when they aren't.

Energizing for Not Breaking Rules Does Not Cause Students to Break Rules

You may be having a "Yeah, but..." moment here:

"Yeah, but...how will she learn what she did wrong and correct it?"

"Yeah, but...aren't I condoning it if I don't correct it?"

"Yeah, but...nobody really talks to kids this way in the real world, and my job is to prepare them for the real world!"

For many teachers, the idea of praising students for what they are *not* doing is, at first, met with disbelief. If you are concerned that students will think that being acknowledged for following the rules is ridiculous, you're not alone, but others who have this concern and try the technique anyhow are usually amazed at how beautifully students respond to it.

If they come from a behavior management perspective, they often misperceive this approach as a "prompting behavior." Behaviorists believe that if you tell a child *not* to do something, you're prompting them to do it. For example, if I tell Tom not to hit his sister, and he then turns and hits her, I've prompted Tom to hit.

When we look through the Nurtured Heart lens at the energetic reality of the situation, and we see that when we 'accuse' kids of not breaking the rules, we are epitomizing the stand of relentlessly energizing the positive. If we do it with genuine appreciation, honesty and gratitude, it has the opposite effect behaviorists might expect. This kind of acknowledgement goes beyond behavioral compliance to effectively impact inner wealth. It inspires the child to begin to see himself as someone who has the greatness of self-control, and who is valued for this greatness.

Before jumping in, educators often express fears about how such statements will be received. "My students are going to laugh at me when I try to do this positivity thing with them," teachers will say. They ll say, "What's this new thing you're trying to do? Did you learn some new trick to keep us in line?" Many teachers considering this shift are afraid that their students will see it as dishonest—that they'll resist being spoken to in such positive ways, and that they will reject the approach wholesale.

Yes, you're learning some new tricks, but they aren't about keeping anyone in line. They are tools to help you live your mission as an educator: to bring out what is the best and most hopeful for every student.

Notching It Up in the Face of Resistance

Most of us are used to operating within the dynamic tension of upside-down energy. Although it might be stressful, it is, at least, predictable. Intense, difficult students know how to get energized connection, and they come to count on this as a way of reinforcing their existence and importance to their favorite toy in the classroom.

For this reason, many will resist the shift you're trying to enact in your classroom as they learn the new rules of engagement and the new status quo. Expect this. Celebrate it as evidence that the child is feeling the shift as real and tangible. **Know that they need to test in order to trust that this shift is truly infused into the culture of the classroom and in you: the teacher as favorite toy.**

Some may require more convincing than others, and that means holding on to those first two stands as though your life depended on it. It means *notching it up* instead of letting yourself be derailed by resistance. As you align with this stand, and you are met you testing, resistance or even mockery by the students, try responses like these:

"Wow! You are an excellent observer. You have noticed I'm trying something new. Very astute."

"Yep, I'm learning to really see what you are doing right not just what you're doing wrong. You're obviously paying close attention. Thanks for bringing this up for the whole classroom!"

"Yes, I've learned that I constantly notice what you're doing wrong, and that I'm really good at talking about that. I've decided that I'd rather talk about what you're doing right. Don't worry, you'll get used to it. I think I will, too."

"Thanks for noticing that I'm trying something new. I see that it makes you feel uncomfortable. Thanks for handling your discomfort with great integrity."

Aligning Intention and Purpose

If we truly intend to cultivate success in our classrooms, we must make sure our intentions are congruent with our purpose. If our purpose is to create success, we need to be warrior-like in identifying and verbally acknowledging what is going well. **The intense child who is *not* acting out *is successful.***

Think about the most impulsive child you know. In the past, you have probably consistently noticed her impulsive acts, and in trying to create an environment where that child won't be triggered or tempted. When she has finally given in to temptation of breaking a rule, your impulse has likely been to focus on getting the child "back on track." But think about what happens *before* this exchange.

As a formerly difficult child, I can tell you that intense children constantly contemplate breaking rules. It is in these moments of deliberation that educators have the power to provide evidence of their success at not breaking the rules. This is where the magic happens. Once the child has accumulated successful moments, he begins to connect the dots. He begins to focus on maintaining success.

In order for this to work, the line between a rule followed and a rule broken needs to be absolutely clear. For most educators, this will require a rule re-vamp not a standardized set of rules for all, but a gentle tweak of whatever rules you already have in place. Let's begin by looking at your classroom rules.

Notching it Up!

List the rules of your classroom below. Be thorough. If you have children at home, feel free to include the rules you observe there as well. Use the extra sheets in the back of this book if your require more space.

If you're like most modern educators, your rules are stated in positive language: *Be kind. Keep your hands to yourself. Be respectful.* And while the idea of positive rules seems key to creating an atmosphere of positivity, this is rarely the case in practice.

Boundaries drawn by positive rules are fuzzy and invite argument. Rules are far more clear when stated in *negative* language. **Each rule should begin with the word "No."** Clarity is key for finding ways to reinforce rules when they are being followed. Where's the line between respect and disrespect? How many arguments have you had with children over whether they've kept their hands to themselves or not?

Look at the rules you wrote in the last journaling box. If they are stated in positive language, can you see how this creates vagueness that invites the pushing of boundaries and arguments about what constitutes a broken rule…and how it invites warnings and lectures instead of effective consequences?

Our culture is focused on manners and politeness. We mistakenly believe that by saying, "Please stop yelling," "Please put your assignments on your desk," or "Please go back to your seat," we're conveying respect. And with a less intense child, this might work. But if I am an intense child, it is my M.O. to constantly test to see where the line is. A choice is implied when adults begin a request with "Please " or "Will you" and energetically, the door is opened to a power struggle. To the difficult child, this is like striking gold!

An ideal rule lets everyone knows where the line is. *No cursing. No name-calling. No hitting. No pushing. No talking back. No refusing to do class work.* Once this line is drawn, students have a choice: to stay on the side of following it or to cross to the other side.

The fact is that students always have that choice. As the adult in the room, you have the power to acknowledge and appreciate them for following rules instead of rewarding them with energized relationship when they do *not* follow them. When students choose to stay on the rule-following side of the line, they can be recognized for using their self-control and power. They end up feeling empowered by their choices to follow the rules.

Discussing the New Rules With Students

You don't have to make a point of introducing the new rules to make the shift into Creative Recognition, although you can do so if that feels right to you. Students are not likely to mind when you 'accuse' them of *following* a classroom rule they didn't know about. And in this approach, the reset IS the consequence for a broken rule. The purpose **is to return students to time-in as quickly as possible after a rule is broken.** Once students understand this, they won't take issue with receiving a consequence, even for breaking a rule they didn't know existed. As the emotional payoffs for following rules become more compelling, students become experts at NOT breaking rules.

Children best experience and integrate rules during time-in. This is an unshakable tenet of the Nurtured Heart Approach. With Proactive Recognition, we are able to create more opportunity for energizing success. Even when a student is upset, something is always going well. Accuse the child of success at the very moment when the child IS truly being successful.

"Julio, I see you're still upset because you did not get your way. I want to accuse you of having great integrity. Even though you are very upset, you are not being disrespectful or rude. You're holding it together, and that is a hard thing to do when you're upset."

"Marie, I want to accuse you of being responsible with your words. You are angry with Justin and you're choosing not to use bad language or disrespect. You are being mature."

For a younger child: "Jacob, I saw that Marty just took the glue from you. Instead of grabbing it back, you stopped yourself and reset, and then used your words to ask for it back. You were being powerful in that moment."

"Jeremy, the teacher just said to stop working and go to the next center, and even though you weren't finished yet, you went to the next center without melting down or even complaining. I am accusing you of being flexible."

The key is to acknowledge what could be happening *right now* that isn't, and to hold that up as the truth in the moment.

"But Isn't That Just Like Letting Them Get Away With It?"

If this question is coming up for you at this juncture, know you're not alone. As teacher, you're wired to...well...teach! As part of the common belief system that is the context of teacher-student relationships, you may have come to believe that *every moment is a teaching moment.* If you let yourself refuse to energize the negative, aren't you letting important teaching moments slip by?

It may seem this way at first, and your hesitancy is understandable. Your discernment here is part of *your* greatness. Trust in it and continue to experiment. I don't hold an intention to convince you of anything here—this is *your* learning curve! Use the energy that comes up around doubts and worries to fuel your ongoing experimentation with these techniques. We hope you come to see that Proactive Recognitions use aligned energy as opposed to "upside-down" energy to anchor what you've tried to convey all along.

Besides, basic rules are pretty standard from school to school, from culture to culture and from generation to generation. Most school-aged children know the rules without being told what they are. At sporting events, the rules aren't posted for the players; they just get a quick penalty when one is broken. When driving, the rules of the road aren't posted on your dashboard; you just get a ticket when you forget to follow them.

Notching it Up!

If you do intend to take time to explain the new rules to your students, use the space below to jot down what you plan to say:

Negative rules create a huge field of possibility in ways that rules can be followed which, in turn, gives you vast possibilities for positive recognition. Let's take, for example, the rule "No hitting." There's no wiggle room: if the student has hit someone else, a rule has been broken, and a consequence is needed. If you are truly in the moment, and if the student hasn't hit even if she is just about to take a swing at someone she is following the rules, and can be recognized for this. What is the truth of the moment? "Sarah, you look like you so want to hit Jennifer, but you haven't. That is a great choice and hard to do when you're angry. That's your wisdom in action."

Still raising an eyebrow about the idea of recognizing a child who is about to hit for not hitting? Remember that Proactive Recognition is just one more way to create dynamic tension. It hinges on the absolute truth of the moment, so there is never any fabrication—just a choice to see in this miraculous way.

It doesn't work on its own; it has to be coupled with the other techniques for providing consistent emotional nutrition during time-in, as well as the refusal to energize negativity. Adding the reset will draw this dynamic tension to its most effective level.

Remember that your energy is the most compelling forcefield in the room, and that you get to choose what to energize. You can choose to walk down a dismal city street and notice the beautiful trees and flowers. You can choose, on a day that is going badly, to notice what's going well, even if the weight of what's going badly seems far greater. And yes, you can choose to notice and acknowledge a child who's about to break a rule for not having done so yet.

At the same time, clear rules starting with "No" help set the stage for effective consequences. This clarity will enable you to give an un-energized reset or time-out as soon as the line is crossed.

Notching it Up!

Re-state your classroom rules using negative language. Try to craft each rule starting with the word "No..."

To give a Proactive Recognition, be on the lookout for students who are *not* breaking rules. Pick one or more students to energize for one or more specific rules being followed. Verbally describe what you see in the context of your classroom rules, giving the child complete credit for her choice to follow the rule in question. Reflect desirable values and qualities of greatness demonstrated by the child in the moment.

For example: "Chris, I see you focusing on your work. Your eyes are busy reading, you are not bothering your neighbor and you are working hard. You are following all the rules. That is what a great student does!" Or, to a group: "Table One, I want to accuse all of you of being on task, discussing the materials without getting distracted and participating in the project. You're showing great leadership right now." Or to the class: "Boys and girls, raise your hand if you are in your seat, your books are opened to page 52 and you are working hard. Give yourself an energetic high-five for being an awesome student. You all are following all the rules and I tremendously value that." If we really and truly value students who are observing the rules, appreciations like these are not hard to come up with!

Stop thinking of rule-breaking as a problem to solve or an issue to avoid. What we energize, grows. The problem-solving, problem-avoiding mindset tends to bring more problems or cause existing problems to snowball. Instead, shine your energy into moments where problems *aren't*.

"Jenna, I see that you are not talking with your neighbor while I'm explaining the assignment. You're being respectful. Thanks for that."

"Malcolm, thanks for following our rule about not getting out of our seats until the bell rings. I can see you're feeling really fidgety, and you're showing us all how powerful you are by staying seated."

Don't use Proactive Recognitions to regain control, manage behavior or passively shame an off-task child. Do spread recognitions evenly throughout your classroom. Any child who is not breaking a rule is fair game.

In the old modes of classroom discipline, your habit might have been to tensely wait and watch without comment as a child starts to misbehave, hoping silently that the child won't go there. That approach leaves you fundamentally powerless to stop the runaway train before it gets started. Instead, start to watch for those moments where the earliest movement toward acting-out is happening. Make it far more interesting for the child to stay in that place or to shift into reverse, away from rule-breaking behaviors. As the child follows that energy, give him or her all the credit for choosing to do so.

"Henry, your face looks angry and I can see you are not wanting to share the blocks with Jared. Yet, you're keeping your cool—you're not hitting, grabbing or pushing anyone, and you aren't ruining Jared's game by knocking his block tower over. What an awesome job you're doing of feeling your angry feelings and keeping others safe at the same time."

"Juanita, you look like you're having a rough time with the assignment, but you haven't tried to look at anyone else's paper. You're showing me how honest and honorable you are."

1. Write down some target behaviors in your classroom rules that tend to get broken.

2. Write down Proactive Recognitions to use when those rules are NOT being broken.

3. Experiment with these for one week.

4. Once the week is up, return here and record your successes below.

Notch It Up: Critical Thinking/Greatness Thinking

If you are conditioned to find problems and solve them, you may initially feel as though you are having to force positive commentary through clenched teeth. For the critical thinker, giving Experiential and Proactive Recognitions will inevitably bring resistance and second-guessing about how these techniques can work as ways to teach academics. When in doubt, the critical thinker is likely to default to a traditional, punitive framework.

For most of us, this conditioning comes from early in our lives. The critical thinking habit can hold powerful influence over the way we see the world and the way we interact with each other and with ourselves. To address this, take some time to think about your own critical-thinking habits and your own resistance to creating a more positive environment in your classroom and in your life. Welcome this process of trying the approach, second-guessing and defaulting to old ways. This is your own testing process in action, and testing is often necessary for real, lasting change.

Are you critical toward your students and coworkers? If so, you are probably equally (if not more) critical toward yourself. Does this describe your current awareness? If so: *congratulations!* Awareness is half of transformation. Once you see the pattern in yourself, you can consciously decide to be less critical and more accepting of yourself. *There is no way you can expect a child with little inner wealth and even less life experience to accept this level of relationship and engagement with you if you do not believe you are worthy of it.*

Bless and release yourself in each moment you spend being self-critical or self-defeating. Reset yourself to the next moment by acknowledging your new level of self-awareness and deciding to create a new pattern.

I have worked with many gifted teachers who reset themselves openly and fearlessly in front of their students. It goes something like this: As students grow increasingly restless and the teacher becomes frustrated, he consciously stops, mid-sentence, and says, "I just need to take a moment to reset." He closes his eyes, takes a few slow deep breaths, and then opens his eyes. He then acknowledges his students for also resetting the energy in the classroom and for now being focused and engaged. The entire process takes about one minute.

Now that you have clarity about your old patterns around critical thinking, you get to choose a different way. What you are really doing here is applying your critical thinking skills to finding what is going right and describing this in detail. Keep reminding yourself how difficult it is when children break rules and keep breaking them in an effort to keep the energy flowing between them and the adults in their lives. As you make conscious choices to create that energetic flow in response to positive choices, let genuine gratitude guide your recognitions. Be grateful to yourself for your willingness to use the energy of critical thinking to create encouragement and appreciation.

Technique #4: *Creative Recognition*

Demonstrate that energized connection is readily available in exchange for complying with requests.

As practitioners of the Nurtured Heart Approach, we strongly believe that clear rules and immediate consequences are paramount to successful implementation. When administered as intended, this is a very strict approach. Sometimes teachers get confused about how to implement at this juncture, because we have spent so much time discussing the importance of creating successes and refusing to energize negativity. Our intention at this point is to become evermore clear and purposeful in *how* we cultivate relationships with our students. When it comes to broken rules, we need to also be very clear.

Every adult has had the experience of making a request of a child and having the child refuse. Simple, minor requests to brush teeth, climb down from a tree, stay seated, complete an assignment or turn off the TV and come to dinner can quickly turn into a showdown. Refusals like these are often attempts to perpetuate the established pattern of and prolonged and energized connection.

Creative Recognitions—also called Photoshop Moments, in honor of the amazing modern technology that allows us to alter and tweak photos in nearly infinite ways—lend even more power in finding and pointing out greatness in students. They *guarantee* compliance and success. If Proactive Recognition puts the rope at the bottom of Shamu's pool, Creative Recognition puts not one rope down there, but many. With this technique, we put rope *everywhere.* The creativity comes in as we make compliance impossible to avoid.

Creative Recognition involves making a request of a student in a way that makes non-compliance impossible. Then, we give all the credit to the student, reflecting how his greatness is expressed through the choice he has made. To give a Creative Recognition, start by making a request that the student can't refuse. If Emma is already in the door of the classroom and on her way to her seat, request that she come in and start toward her spot in the room. If David is hanging his backpack on one of the hooks outside the classroom, request that he hang up his backpack. The key is to **catch the child in the middle of following a direction, being productive or performing a requested or desired function.**

Make requests in clear, firm language. Avoid giving the child any impression that he has a choice by asking ("Would you..." "Could you..." "Will you please..."). Any request that starts with with "Please..." or "Will you..." opens the energetic door to a power struggle. To the difficult child, this is like striking gold because historically non-compliance leads to heightened relationship and connection, albeit negative!

Make your request as a statement:

- ✓ As Thomas sits down and pulls out his class notebook: "Thomas, I need you to take your seat and get ready to start taking notes." Then, once you see that he has finished what he started: "Wow, Thomas, you're already there. Thanks for your initiative. You walked right in and got ready to learn. What a great example you're setting."
- ✓ As Bonnie starts to collect her paper scraps to throw away: "Bonnie, please gather up your paper scraps." Give her a few seconds to continue, then: "I see you're being really careful not to leave any trash behind. You obviously care about the condition of our classroom! And now I see you tossing the scraps in the recycling bucket, which shows that you also are conscious of keeping as much waste out of the landfill as possible. If more people were like you, I think the earth would be in a much healthier state than it is right now."

This technique works magic with children who are resisting the approach and doing all they can to get back to the old way of extracting relationship around negativity. You are literally hijacking them into success and then giving them a taste of what it's like to be energized for their choice to surrender to their greater selves.

Notching it Up! *Consider the following scenarios. Craft a Creative Recognition that might work for each situation.*

Four-year-old Marina has a habit of throwing sand at other children in the preschool sandbox. You find her playing there with three other children, using a shovel to fill a pail. You say:

Ten-year-old Malcolm is well-known for his oppositional habits. If he can say "no" to any request, he will do it without a second thought, and he'll happily engage in an extended debate in the minutes that follow his refusal. One day, you see him in an animated conversation with another student. He seems excited and happy. You say:

Fifteen-year-old Tereza is growing up too fast. All of her teachers are worried about her. She dresses in revealing clothes, wears a lot of makeup, and is constantly seen flirting with boys. In class one day, she sits with her head down, reading and scribbling notes in her notebook. You say:

The focus of Creative Recognition is to relentlessly find ways to "pause the footage" of a child's life, even on his worst day, and to fearlessly accuse him of being online with the tasks, responsibilities and requests that are present and ongoing. Not just of being good: being *great.* There is no single right answer here. That's why this technique is called *Creative* Recognition!

This method gives you the ability to applaud responsibilities and requests that are, in even the slightest sense, being met. Some of those molecules are moving in the right direction:

"Jacob, I love that you are following the directions and responsibilities of being a great student in this class, and I didn't even have to ask today. You are seated and ready to learn, well-groomed and alert to getting started with our lesson. Thank you for being so respectful to my expectations."

Weaving Recognitions Into Class Time

Allow recognitions to happen seamlessly within class time. Strongly and intensely begin to energize the positive, but do so "on the fly" as you teach curriculum. Howard compares this to walking: academics is one foot and the Nurtured Heart Approach is the other. Once you establish a rhythm that includes both, a captivating dynamic is created in the classroom. Students feel held and supported in an atmosphere of positivity while they learn.

Whenever possible, create opportunities for students to energize each other. Watch the momentum of greatness building.

Pointers for Maintaining the First Two Stands

Notching the approach up to whatever level works is the way to break through the negativity of even the most resistant student. **No matter how tough, resistant, defiant or distant the kid, the way through is more positivity.**

Keep creating situations where the student's competency is guaranteed.

Take time to generate recognitions from your heart. Reset yourself to positivity as often as necessary. Stay clear about the rules. Make new rules as often as you like, and remember to energize students for *not* breaking them. Any time you run out of ideas or energy, refer to Chapter Seven in this book, where you'll find tried-and-true ideas for classroom activities for every grade level.

Notching It Up: *An Approach for Every Student*

This approach is usually adopted in an effort to deal with high rollers in the classroom, but it works best for them and for every student when it is used consistently for the entire class. Even better results come with its use across the whole school.

Selectively applying the approach to certain students who act out often will undermine your efforts. "Good" students will wonder why they're getting the short end of the stick and marginal students will quickly see that getting this new kind of energized connection is as easy as becoming a chronic rule-breaker and boundary-pusher.

If you find that your initial efforts to energize students is backfiring, commit (or re-commit) to delivering energizing statements to every student—even the one who has never broken a rule in your classroom. Gradually increase the intensity of application to meet the needs of every student. In other words: notch it up.

Notching it Up!

Select three students: a high roller, a marginal kid, and a "good" kid. Consider how you could energize them the next time you are all together in the classroom. Use the techniques to formulate a few energizing statements for each, and write them below.

Make a point of using those statements over the next day or two. Then, repeat this exercise with three other students, using the space below or a separate sheet of paper. This mental preparation will get you in the habit of energizing across the behavioral board.

Chapter Six

Nurtured Heart Consequences: *The Time-Out/Reset*

The greatest glory in living lies not in never falling, but in rising every time we fall.
— Nelson Mandela

When you started reading this book, you might have thought of yourself as *plenty* positive; what you really thought you needed were consequences that would actually work. We hope you now see that even the most positive educator has room to notch it up.

And now, having made it through that part of the Nurtured Heart Approach journey, here you are. You've finally made it to the chapter on consequences. So: How do you get a child to do what you want without focusing on disobedience and negative energy? **Say, "That's a reset," and move on to your next positive recognition as quickly as possible.**

Create a pause in the action, drop the rope to the bottom of Shamu's tank and start over. For example: pause; then say, "Eric, I like that you stopped tapping your pencil and distracting your neighbor. Great reset. Now you are engaged and participating. That's what great students do."

One more variation: Emulate the reset of a video game. When a rule is broken, let all energetic charge drop, then start a fresh game. "Reset!" Pause. "Welcome back, Margarita! I love that you are now making great effort toward participating. What color paper would you like?"

You can even reset a child by creating the illusion that the reset has already been completed! This is useful for children accustomed to arguing and power struggles, or who are exceptionally resistant to positive feedback. For example, "Wow, Rhett, I don't even have to reset you, because you reset *yourself*. Now you're back in the game. Welcome back!" Or: "Table three, thanks for showing the class what a great reset looks like! You're back on track and now working as a successful team. If I had a camera I'd take your picture and put it right next to rule number three. Great job!"

Anticipate that some students will already be playing the Nurtured Heart Approach "game" willingly and skillfully in response to the first two Stands (no energy to negativity and relentlessly energizing the positive). They will be acting out their own greatness and energizing other students, and they may even be refusing to break rules.

But the most intense children in your classroom may be going to extremes in reaction to this new dynamic. They want the relationship they're used to—the kind they've grown comfortable with and are skilled at eliciting whenever they like. This new kind of interaction goes against their deeply held expectations of cause and effect.

Notch it Up: Embracing Resistance

Remember: resistance is just another source of energy we can use to fuel greatness. The reset is a way of processing the energy of resistance and purposefully guiding it in the direction of success.

Imagine that the very intense child has been dancing the waltz for years, both at home and at school. She knows the steps without having to think or concentrate. Suddenly, you (an important adult in her life) burst into a country two-step. The rhythm and sound of the music is unfamiliar; the steps feel unpredictable. She may initially try the new dance, but awkwardness will drive her to try to get you engaged in the old, predictable dance, because it is within her comfort zone. You encourage her to keep trying, but she becomes completely focused on getting you back into the more familiar pattern. The stronger her innate intensity, the more intently she tries to go back to the dance she already knows well. Escalation of unwanted behaviors is almost guaranteed.

The intense child will need to test your level of commitment to this approach. Remember, his experience has been that the more resistant he is, the bigger, more involved, and more invested in "changing his behavior" the important adults in his life have become. It will take some time to convince him that this payoff is no longer found there.

Many teachers (and other adults) from the intense child's past have likely tried many different tactics to get these behaviors to go away. He has learned that if he resists for long enough, eventually the adults will give up on the current tactic and move on to another one. **Because his primary motivation is maintaining relationships, the child is more invested in the process of being figured out than in compliance.**

In his resistance, the intense child is also trying to gauge whether you can handle his intensity. (Instead of saying, "Can you hear me now?" he's saying, "Can you *handle* me now?") Being repeatedly celebrated for doing the right thing and receiving an un-energetic reset for every broken rule will answer this question. Once this new kind of relationship becomes predictable, his receptivity will increase. Energy once spent on resistance will be transformed to a commitment to living out his own greatness.

Resistance is a good sign: *you are reaching the child,* and she is recognizing the shift! This is her last hurrah her last-ditch effort to dance the old dance before she surrenders to learning the new one. Notch it up in response: remain relentless and purposeful in delivering clear and energetic connection through active, emotionally nutritious time-in and unceremonious time-out.

Third Stand:

Absolutely CLEAR!

Maintain total clarity about rules and always give resets for rules broken.

The Myth of "Rapport Building"

Most teachers have been taught that engagement and rapport between students and teachers are essential for academic success. These teachers don't believe that they are reaching a student unless the student responds to them in a manner that demonstrates this kind of rapport and trust. Even when students don't appear to be receptive, transformation is taking place. Hold to your Stands even if the child seems to be ignoring you.

Thinking that we must establish relationship prior to teaching implies a lack of the sacred connection that already exists between adult and child. Ultimately, *the ritual of establishing rapport and trust can build barriers to establishing the existing truth of relationship with the child.*

I came to this conclusion while working with juvenile offenders. They were in detention and the court had ordered them to undergo counseling. These were some of the most resistant teens I had ever had the pleasure of knowing. Because they were at the mercy of the court, I never knew whether I would be seeing them more than once, so I took each meeting as an opportunity to have them experience what it is to be seen, heard, honored and cherished for everything that was right and good about them. I did not have the luxury of building trust or rapport, nor did I waste any energy trying to convince them that they *should* trust me. Really, *why should they*?

Instead, *I trusted them* in each moment they were not being destructive, out of control, or disrespectful. I authentically reflected my experience of them in each precious moment. My goal was to plant as many seeds as possible: to have them know what it feels like to be honored, so that they would want more of that in their future. I carried with me the belief that one's life can change in a moment, and I was determined to make the most of each moment with these teens.

And although rapport wasn't a requirement for our therapeutic relationship, we did build wonderful rapport. Being seen and acknowledged in greatness opens up even the most closed of hearts. Many of them continued to check in with me well after they were required to by the courts. Some who are now adults still update me occasionally!

Don't wait until the child seems ready to change. Assume that you have a powerful relationship simply because you are an influential adult in her life. Match her intensity. *POUR* it on. Hang on to your stands like a dog with a bone. Embrace resistance as part of the process.

Notching it Up!

The next time you encounter resistance in the classroom, practice notching it up. Give time-in more of your energy in response to resistance and notch up your commitment to refusing to energize what's wrong. Write about your experience below.

____

____

____

____

____

Consequences: Where the Rubber Meets the Road

Even those who've found the implementation of this approach to be easy may find themselves challenged when moving into implementation of consequences.

Of course it's tough! You're in the process of shedding past beliefs about teaching and classroom management. Although you understand why traditional forms of classroom management are counterproductive to classroom dynamics, you may fall back on this punitive framework when things seem difficult or out of control...the exact juncture at which consequences are needed.

Expect that as you reach a level of mastery with the Nurtured Heart reset, your "high rollers" will begin to perceive that your energy is now a match for theirs. Even as they become more drawn to you, they will also be consumed with testing these new waters until they are certain the old ways no longer work.

A Nurtured Heart Approach consequence is dependent on the vibrancy of the time-in built around the techniques outlined in the last two chapters. Remember the 80/20 rule. **Resets will not work unless upside-down energy has been flipped right-side-up.**

Beginning with resets and abandoning the first two stands will surely backfire! That's why we describe this piece *after* introducing the pieces about creating and energizing success.

When a sturdy foundation of positive acknowledgement is built and the new resolve around no relationship for negativity is established, it's time to add the consequences piece of this approach. If you feel you have not gotten to this point yet, continue to purposefully create successes and refuse to energize negativity. **Continue to use whatever classroom disciplinary methods you have always used, but *remain flat, unattached, and unceremonious* when responding to negative behaviors.**

Bring in the reset when your students seem comfortable with receiving recognitions from you, and you notice they are using the language of recognition amongst each other and toward you. When students feel energized for good choices, resets are seamless and unencumbered with drama or negative energy.

If you begin to give resets as described in this chapter and they do not work, this is a cue that you need to ramp up the positives and look at the ways in which you might be leaking negativity.

Reasons Why Traditional Consequences Don't Work

Difficult children thrive on adversity. Any consequence (or buildup to a consequence) that conveys energy in response to negative behavior will encourage more negative behavior. Lectures, pep talks, warnings, screaming fits, humorous mini-sermons and escalating consequences all give the child YOU when he or she is acting out:

1. **Traditional lectures** (the traditional kind, about what the child is doing wrong) might be difficult for a child to sit through, but he has your attention for as long as it lasts. All it takes for him to amp up the relationship is to argue or break more rules during the lecture. Remember, this is NOT a conscious or calculated decision on the part of the child; she's merely seeking and drawn to energy. A Nurtured Heart lecture about the child's greatness is much more fun and productive for both child and teacher.
2. **Traditional pep talks,** however well-intended, send the wrong message. Although they are framed as positive ("Come on, I know you can do this!"), the energetic message of a pep talk is, "You're not doing very well right now…I know you can do better!" Your energy goes to the child's wrong choices, bad decisions, and the *future possibility* of success.
3. **Warnings** powerfully energize children for negative choices. As they move toward the line between a rule followed and a rule broken, they get their favorite toy's lights blinking and flashing. The closer they get to the line, the better the show. **Warnings given before a rule is broken convey your expectation that the child will break a rule.** This is a major negativity leak. You might as well hold up a sign that says, "If you want relationship with me, break a rule."
4. **Screaming fits** or other high-intensity outbursts are upsetting to both adult and student. And yet, even the best-intentioned, most compassionate adult can be driven to a point where she loses her temper and says or does things she regrets. For the extremely intense child, this isn't a deterrent. The kind of relationship that happens between a student and an educator who has been driven to this point is painful but deep, and there is a certain kind of student that needs this strong a connection. But it will ultimately only widen the existing gap to greatness.
5. **Humorous mini-sermons** may be supported by pure intentions, but they send the wrong message. Sometimes, attempts to deal with boundary-pushing or rule-breaking through joking and play will work. But a pattern of using humor in this way serves as an open invitation to students: "Break a rule or threaten to do so if you want to enjoy fun banter with the most important person in the room."

In summary: **most traditional consequences accidentally deepen the child's impression that more connected relationship is available in exchange**

for pushing boundaries of rules.

Think back to the video game intention in Chapter Three. The brief, clear consequences given by video games are incredibly effective because being *in* the game is so energizing for players. Constant recognition of the energy of success creates a brilliant counterpoint to those brief moments of being *out* of the game. That contrast makes the consequence powerful despite its being brief and non-punitive. If time-in is not clearly established, consequences have little or no impact.

Escalating Consequences, Warning Systems, Redirection, Traditional Time-Outs and Withdrawal of Privileges

Traditional thinking goes like this: when a child breaks rules repeatedly, you keep giving stiffer and stiffer consequences until you have some impact. This thinking is based on the belief that if there is to be an awakening on the part of the child, it will happen in response to a progression of increasingly punitive, drastic consequences. We think: *Somewhere along the line, if I give a serious enough consequence, this child will become afraid enough or suffer enough that he'll wake up and smell the coffee.*

The Nurtured Heart Approach discards this notion mostly, because it's ineffective, as current research into the impact of zero tolerance policies and other harsh disciplinary methods in schools demonstrates. Even for the toughest children, the real awakening is not to the error of one's ways, but *to one's greatness.* Being led to see one's own greatness is the path that truly motivates and inspires and it doesn't call upon educators to compromise the child's well-being with mounting levels of stress and fear.

Any form of **escalating consequences** is an affirmation to students that they can still obtain relationship around negativity. Giving one consequence and then adding more consequences or increasing intensity when the child continues to act out hangs a neon sign that says you're still offering 100-dollar bills for negativity.

In the Nurtured Heart Approach, **the same simple consequence is given for every broken rule, and every consequence is given in the context of a clean slate.** The last time the child broke a rule is not a consideration in the present moment. Each time-out/reset is new and unburdened by deeds done in the past or expectations for the future. In the case of an extreme infraction where someone gets hurt or property is destroyed, the same time-out/reset guidelines apply, but some sort of restitution may be called for once time-in is restored.

School discipline policies often involve some version of warnings: Turning the Card, Losing a Pillar or Changing the Traffic Light are a few examples we've seen in schools. They are intended to give the child fair warning that they are edging toward the line and will soon have a consequence or a trip to the principal's office (which is, by the way, yet another reward to the intense child). Some schools start each child off with a certain number of points, from which deductions are taken throughout class time. Consequences are held in store for students who lose a certain number of points. As formerly intense children, we can tell you from experience that this system might as well be called "Game ON!"

If your school has such policies in place and you are unable to discard them for your classroom, you can still implement the Nurtured Heart Approach. Just remember to very purposefully and intentionally build time-in and make resets your first response to rule-breaking, before reverting to the school's standard system of consequences. Before long, the standard system is likely to become obsolete.

Redirection is initiated by the caregiver or teacher to distract the child from a potentially difficult situation and get them involved in another activity. The problem is, the child quickly figures out that the way to get nurturance from a caring adult is to break a rule!

Traditional time-outs—where a child is sent to a special spot to sit for a period of time, usually the number of minutes matching her age—are a step toward withdrawing energy from negativity (if you can actually get a one-year-old to sit still for one minute or a three-year-old to sit still for three minutes, that is). *What's missing is a corresponding time-in.*The effectiveness of time-out is amplified many-fold when the child has a vibrant time-in to look forward to.

Traditional time-outs are often surrounded on all sides by energy to negativity: warnings beforehand, relationship around getting the child into time-out, and then sometimes a lecture afterward to ensure that the child knows what he's done wrong and to request that he not do it again. It's not uncommon for the teacher to facilitate a formal apology to the wronged party, which gives the child further evidence that the juiciest time-in happens within the context of broken rules. All of these factors drain the effectiveness of the consequence.

Withdrawing privileges is really just another kind of time-out. It requires foresight, organization and follow-through from the educator. And there are children who, when faced with withdrawal of privileges, will shrug their shoulders and hold an "I don't care" attitude, which leaves the educator powerless.

Sometimes it seems easiest to combine the warning with the withdrawal of privileges: "If you don't do __________, then you won't get to__________." This sets up a dynamic where the child is not truly motivated to do the right thing—she only does it because you have dangled a carrot in front of her nose. And if the child cares more about energized relationship with you than she does about the carrot, the consequence will be ineffective.

Consequences that are *enforced* require the giver of the consequence to *force* the child to comply; in that very process of forcing (or attempting to force) compliance, much energy is given to negativity. This is the point at which many of us get pulled into the myth that if the consequence is big enough, the behavior will stop. We ratchet up the consequences in the hopes that the child or adolescent will learn the lesson. By now, you can see the error in this way of thinking.

The Nurtured Heart time-out distills the foundation of time-out—removal from action, from fun, from learning, from *relationship*—that is the basis of every consequence. It gives an illusion of a consequence: a pause in the action when a rule is broken and a wide-open door back to time-in. Your role is to *hit the pause button* and demonstrate to the child in the very next moment that success is happening, and that you will offer energized relationship around that success.

Teens Need Intense Relationships With Adults Too

Many who work with teenagers will argue against implementing the Nurtured Heart Approach by saying that teens don't care about relationship with educators—that they are much more invested in peer acceptance, cell phones or video games.

I have found that many teens *seem* to have given up on their relationships with adults, and have turned to peers for the guidance and mentorship they need. If adults are not available for positive interaction, they will continue to seek out negativity and adversity in those relationships. The energetic benefits outweigh the liabilities of consequences for rule-breaking and challenging behaviors. But when offered strong guidance from adults, they are always available to it.

How To Give a Reset

When a rule is broken, remove the gift of yourself. Choose your own "reset word" or hand signal. Try "chill," "pause," "freeze," or "take a moment," or some other creative variation on this theme.

The reset works best if felt from the heart, intuitively. This mode of consequencing is not about behavior management it's about changing school culture. Still, your school may require that you describe a procedure for resets. Here s the procedure, if you need one:

When giving a reset, take the following steps: Reset, Restore, and Recover.

1. **Reset: Say, "[Name], that's a time-out" or "[Name], reset"** or something similar. **Energetically and/or physically turn away.** *Turn off* the relationship. Remember, YOU decide how much energy you will radiate in this moment. Be prepared for the intense child to up the ante at this point. He may get bigger and louder in an attempt to get more from you. **It is *crucial* that you refuse to give the child energy at this moment.** Stop the energetic flow between you and the student.
2. **Restore: End the reset as soon as the rule-breaking stops.** As soon as there is any shift in the child's behavior toward following rules, restore the child to time-in with a verbal welcome-back (more on this below).
3. **Recover/Restart:** The moment the child has stopped the negative behavior, it's time to create time-in. *Jump on it!* What can the child be recognized for?

That's the reset. Convey the sense that a momentary consequence has been administered just long enough to allow for an opportunity to appreciate the child for no longer breaking the rules. Stay in the truth of this very moment: "I so appreciate the wisdom you're showing in your choice not to argue. You have the greatness of being able to reset even when you're frustrated."

The reset can happen in as little as a couple of seconds. It can happen in an instant! If another rule is broken right away, guess what happens? Another reset. **Withhold any inkling of emotional attachment to the child's staying out of reset.** Whether the video game avatar gets blown up once or a hundred times, the game's response remains exactly the same. One moment, the toy is putting on a great show; and then, suddenly, batteries out...and then, again, right back in.

All the while, stay in the truth of each moment. You love the child unconditionally throughout the process of the reset, but you are momentarily unavailable when the reset is taking place.

Here's an example of a brilliant reset. A mother is learning the approach at home with her preschool-aged son. The child goes to the refrigerator, takes out the milk, and intentionally spills it all over the floor.

The standard mindset on this is that this is a serious offense that merits a serious verbal response. We can't let this child get away with something like this! Right? And of course we've got to get in there with the towels to wipe up that spill *right away*, because the day this oppositional child cleans up after himself will be the day pigs fly...upside down and backwards. So much to say and so little time...and all the while, tons of energy and relationship for negativity.

Here's how it plays out. The child kicks his mom and runs away from her. The mom tells the child to reset, then turns her back on him and begins to talk quietly and casually to her husband, who is sitting at the kitchen table (not quite sold on the approach yet, but willing to play along). The child fusses for a while, spits on the floor, yells (sometimes loudly), but she absolutely refuses to give him any energy. This goes on for quite a while.

And then, because he can't seem to get anything out of her with his tried-and-true machinations, he heads for the towel drawer. He gets out some towels...and he begins to clean the spill up himself!

Immediately, his mom pours out BIG energy in response to his positive choice. She turns around, gets in his space, looks him in the eye, gets present and powerful, and launches into a torrent of highly energized verbal appreciation. She lets him know how great it was that he found a way to reset himself without her help, and otherwise creates a vibrant time-in filled with the truth of the moment: his important decision to not break any rules in this moment, and to be cooperative and thoughtful about cleaning up. Her son perceives this new relational, energetic truth as far more engaging than the energetic vacuum of time-out.

After repeated experiences like this, and a consistent experience of time-in whenever rules aren't being broken, the child stops wanting to be reset. He knows that getting Mom's energy doesn't require rule-breaking, tantrums or spilled milk. On the contrary, the boy learns that following the rules consistently works to get MORE of the adults in his life. He comes to like being the child who uses good judgement. As his inner wealth builds, he comes to cherish his positive choices and his greatness continues to blossom. This intense child is now intense about being *great.*

Successful Resets In the Classroom

To create successful resets in the classroom:

Remember: ***you are the prize.***

Sometimes, newcomers to the approach will say, "But I don't *want* to be the prize." Guess what? You don't have a choice. You signed up to be the gift of energy, connection and relationship. This is the reality of being a teacher.

Get crystal-clear about the rules.

Review your rules as often as necessary, but also know that you can give a reset for a rule you didn't think of until someone broke it.

No CSI (Crime Scene Investigation).

When you reset a student, *do not* explain the reason for the reset. Yes you read it right! That explanation will only feed negativity and pass out energetic "cash."

Welcome the child back to time-in as quickly as possible.

As soon as you've welcomed the child back to time-in, call her out about ways she's now being successful and following the rules. You can include a Proactive Recognition of her choice to follow whatever rule was broken prior to the reset.

Here's an example: "Ally, welcome back. Thank you for looking at your workbook and finding the answer. You are following the rules and being a conscientious student." If the child has been reset for breaking a new rule, use Proactive Recognition to explain it in the context of time-in.

What If the Child is *Really* Rule-Breaking?

A common question heard in Nurtured Heart trainings is: "What if the kid is doing something really serious? If this child hits someone, or destroys property, or cheats on a test, I'm supposed to just give this little 'reset' and let her get away with it?"

Do these provocative questions bring up any response in you? Notice that response. Are you finding that these questions have been on your mind since beginning this chapter? Maybe the idea of a non-punitive, very brief consequence has rankled you since you first opened this book.

If it does, you're still caught up in a punitive mindset. This is understandable, because this mindset is deeply entrenched in most traditions and cultures. It shows up in parenting, correctional systems (the notion that giving stiffer jail sentences is more likely to act as a deterrent or change behavior), even organized religion.

Of course, if you are facing a challenge that you really should not or cannot handle in the classroom, school policy and safety take precedence, whether they come from a punitive mindset or not. But in most situations, the punitive mindset dictates that a consequence is more effective when it's longer, more drastic, or more frightening. *The truth is that escalating consequences in response to escalating misbehavior doesn't stop the escalation.* **If anything, it feeds the fire we're trying to put out.**

Our belief that a more punitive consequence will make the child learn more or change more quickly is not founded in reality. A child doesn't learn more in an hour-long consequence than in a short reset. What does happen is stress, resentment and a commitment to further manifest the behavior that earned the consequence in the first place. **Creating more distress in a child by escalating consequences does not correlate to increased awareness for that child.** It doesn't create cognitive-behavioral learning. The only benefit is that the educator feels as though he's meted out an appropriate dose of justice!

Recent brain research tells us why the punitive approach to consequences fails as a teaching tool. When children are distressed, their brains become hyperstimulated. Their limbic brains take over, and while in this fight-or-flight mode, they can't learn or retain information. Learning occurs through a non-punitive method that recognizes the power inherent in the energy of relationship and the choice about where and when that energy is expressed. The awakening we seek occurs when we recognize those times when problems aren't happening.

From Fight-or-Flight to Calm and Centered

When a child is stuck in a "negative portfolio" an idea of herself as always in trouble she is in a constant state of nervous system arousal. The same goes for students who have been labeled as difficult, learning disabled or behaviorally disordered. For these students, school is a source of anxiety and fear. In this state of anxiety, she finds it difficult or impossible to build healthy relationships or to learn or retain information.

In response to either giving or receiving a compliment, a high-dose surge of dopamine and norepinephrine (two neurotransmitters with relaxant, mood-elevating effects) moves into the front temporal lobes of the brain. Excess stress causes confused, distorted thinking, compromises short-term memory, and impairs communication between the left 'thinking' brain and the right 'emotional' brain. When a student has a history of trauma, which many difficult children do, the extent of this stress response is greater. He will think less clearly, react more viscerally, and harbor more fear and aggression than a classmate who has not suffered a traumatic event.

When we create an inner wealth-enhancing environment of safety, healthy relationship and loving connection, these children can learn to relax while in school. Their brain chemistry shifts in ways that make them more capable of learning, remembering and healthy interpersonal interaction.

Teachers have demonstrated enormous creativity with resets. One teacher working with children in a group home setting found that paper reset "forms" worked best for these kids. When in trouble, these kids became overwhelmed, and the reset forms helped them to take their resets in chunks.

The greatest impact of the reset comes with the restoration that follows: the kiss of forgiveness. "Justin, I love that you're sitting there being mature. You aren't fighting with Julia. Now I see you're going to do some working out on your pull-up bar—that's a great use of your energy." Time-in!

Resets delivered in this way convey that:

✓ Your students are capable of following the rules

✓ Your students are capable of recovering after breaking a rule

✓ You do not fear that your students will break rules

✓ You will fearlessly enforce the rules, *every time*

✓ You are committed to staying in the moment, not the past or the future

✓ You are completely available to them within the context of rules NOT broken

In Resets, Your Students Can Trust...

...that they will receive consistent, predictable consequences carrying no energetic charge whatsoever. They also learn to trust that resets will always lead back to an energized time-in, where they'll be confronted with irrefutable evidence of their successes.

The Nurtured Heart time-out, like a video game consequence, is unemotional. Video games don't get cranky and change the rules or fly off the handle in response to one player's decisions on Monday and let the same thing go on Tuesday. There's never a random day where you have to get to level 28 before you start accruing points. And video games don't let things slide that would be major infractions on other days just because they're in a good mood. Above all, video games are *consistent*, and so are Nurtured Heart resets: they are *always* given in response to a broken rule, and are always immediately followed by a return to time-in.

Immediate time-in following a reset is vitally important to both the child and the adult. The adult stays in the moment and refuses to live in the past, making time-in so much more compelling than time out and sending an inspiring message: *there is always a way to start over.*

As children become used to this new system of consequences, they find recovery is inevitable. Just as resets are a certainty, so is the return to time-in. They come to recognize that rule-breaking does not dictate how much their educators care for them, attend to them, value them or appreciate them. Instead, they have experiences of being held in esteem when they are not breaking rules, as well as experiences of failing to have negative choices energized.

Notching it Up: *The Courage to Reset Yourself*

So, here's the elephant in the living room...What if you are *really* frustrated or angry with a child who has been especially challenging all day? What if that child breaks a rule and responds to your reset with a refusal? What if she continues to test? And what about those moments where a reset has been completed, but you are still simmering with anger and feel like doing anything but welcoming the child back (preferring, perhaps, to make them *pay* for ruining your lesson, being disrespectful, or breaking a rule)?

These are the moments where the rubber truly meets the road. **If you are hanging on to anger, you are feeding negativity, and the pattern of testing will continue.**

Silently acknowledge your anger or frustration, energize yourself for handling it without lecturing or scolding, and *use the energy of that anger* as "rocket fuel" to move both you and that child to the next moment, where anger and frustration no longer rule the day. In other words: **give yourself a reset and energize yourself in the new moment of time-in.** When you create a pause and move into the next moment in a clear way, the child will too.

Notching it Up!

Think about your most intense, most difficult student or students. Imagine a particular situation that made you angry or frustrated. Recall it clearly and feel the feelings that came up when you were in the thick of that situation.

Now, acknowledge that what you are experiencing is not good or bad, not positive or negative. It's just energy. And for most of us, the energy of anger and frustration is BIG! Feel it in your body...and then, channel that energy toward some aspect of greatness, either in yourself or in one of the students whose behavior has been the source of your frustration.

Write about this experience below.

Get Back to Time-In (As Quickly as Possible)

Once a time-out has been given, make it your goal to get that child back to time-in as quickly as possible. ***Always* end a reset by giving the child a 'welcome back to time-in' acknowledgement!**

When it's time to end a reset, mightily resist:

- ✓ Launching into lecture mode (unless you are lecturing the child about how he's now following the rules or being successful in some other way)
- ✓ Trying to get the child to apologize for breaking the rule (this energizes negativity, and besides, it's over and you're on to the current moment, when the rule is *not* being broken)

Your commitment to finding the slightest break in the rule-breaking action to welcome the child back to time-in completes the structure of the approach. Ultimately, even the most intense child will find it impossible to avoid success!

Expect to Be Tested...

Howard likes to say, "When you put a new roof on a house, you want it to rain." So it is with the new structure of rewards and consequences that comes with the Nurtured Heart Approach.

When you introduce the reset in your classroom, students will test it. To maintain your sanity, let go of the assumption that your job is to prevent students from breaking rules. Let go of any emotional investment you have in their choices to break the rules of your classroom. Get out of the way and let them exhaust all of their ploys, excuses and machinations.

Easier said than done, right? Yes, and it will go more smoothly if you remain tuned in to your need to reset yourself to the next moment when things get tough. Be willing to energize yourself throughout the day. Refuse to be attached to the outcome of anything.

You cannot keep anyone from breaking the rules, especially your students. In the end, your belief that you have control over your students is an illusion! Yes, we all have fairly particular codes of conduct to live by, but ultimately, we all still have the freedom to break any rule at any time! Kids are aware of this—even the cooperative ones. It's incumbent on us to learn for ourselves that life is sweeter when we don't break the rules. Besides: we all mess up from time to time, even when we try to be perfect. To keep the faith throughout this testing period, remind yourself as often as necessary that rules *not* broken are successes realized.

The journey to right-side-up energy in the classroom can seem arduous at first. Keep in mind that each new moment is a new chance to get it right. **This approach is *not* about perfection.** Remember that this is a process; know you will slip up! Reset when this happens, then return to acting and responding with intention, not out of reactivity. Reset yourself as necessary, even in front of your students; or request a communal reset for the whole room if that feels right.

Students whose teachers make a practice of resetting themselves learn an invaluable lesson that isn't included in any academic curriculum: that challenges (including challenging emotions) are a given for everyone, and that *there is always space to begin again*. What a beautiful gift to give your students!

You get to stay in your power in an unerringly positive way, while also empowering the child. Refusal to give warnings ahead of time or to engage in "Crime Scene Investigation" after a rule is broken progressively deepens students' concepts of themselves as people who are capable of following the rules, and as people who can recover following a choice to break one of those rules.

The Nurtured Heart reset gives students the perception that they are: (a) being held accountable, and (b) missing out on time-in.

Eventually, children exposed consistently to this approach start to self-navigate. They begin to make their own rules and consequences and to reset themselves. Imagine how much curriculum you'll be able to cover once this happens, and how joyful a place your classroom will become.

Introducing the Reset to Students

Some teachers choose to discuss the reset with their students as a part of their classroom discipline procedures. If you decide to present the reset instead of introducing it on the fly, we recommend something along these lines: "From now on, when you break a rule, I'm just going to say your name and 'reset [or whatever word or signal you choose].' (Some teachers will have students put their heads down on their desks or push their chairs back to help them remember who's in a reset.) I'll expect you to sit quietly until I end your reset. I'm not going to lecture you or punish you. I think you'll like this a lot better than the old way."

Do resets on the spot, without requiring the student to move to a new location. A request to a child to go somewhere else for a reset holds the door open for a refusal, which can complicate and escalate the situation. Keep reminding yourself that a reset is really just an *illusion* of a consequence—a break in the action. **The easier you make it for the student to reset, the faster you can get back to time-in, which is the whole point.**

Part of effective implementation of resets is knowing the needs of your students. Very young children or children with sensory issues may need to be removed from an overstimulating environment to be able to reset and start over appropriately. Over time, even children with special needs who initially need to be sent out to reset will be able to reset in the classroom among their peers. I have seen this shift occur in many schools.

The Intense Child and the Reset

An intense child often finds, early in life, that her intensity makes other people uncomfortable. Repeated experiences of others being shocked, angered or driven away by her behaviors cause her to feel insecure about her understanding of what's appropriate—of how much is too much. In implementing the reset, we give the intense child the gift of learning that she *can* handle herself. She can handle her energy, and so can we. The reset helps the intense child figure out, in an experiential way, how she can make it less exhausting for others to be around her. That message comes in a congruent way; she gets *more* when she is not breaking the rules. She no longer feels she has to create rivalry or difficulty to get the attention she needs.

During time-in, *pursue the intense children in your classroom with a greater level of intensity than their pursuit of you*. When you match or exceed their intensity, they relax! "Nail" the problem child before he even walks in the door. Follow those tough kids around the room with the intention of reflecting their positive attributes and choices.

Consider the most intense children in your classroom to be gifts to you. They will demand complete clarity and consistency, and will challenge you at every turn to maintain your Stands; and ultimately help you create a *more* positive experience for every student.

Notching it Up!

Part I: Gratitude is a foundational part of the Nurtured Heart Approach. Write about what you are grateful for: the intense children in your classroom, the good choices they and others make, the qualities of greatness you see and enjoy while you are at work. Let yourself write without censoring; let your gratitude flow.

Part II: How does it feel to experience deep gratitude? Check in with it; savor it; set an intention to remember to go back to this place of gratitude to bring a student back from a reset or to create an authentic, vibrant time-in at any other time. Write your intention below, in your own words.

Helping Children From Destructive Home Environments

A common question in trainings is whether this approach can really help children from abusive or neglectful environments. Can we make a difference for these children?

Yes. In the lives of children with difficult home situations, there is a deep space for relationship with meaningful teachers. Plant seeds in the best way you can. They'll germinate eventually. You are giving that child something he isn't getting anywhere else.

As a difficult kid in Catholic school, I would drop a bomb in class just to be able to pass the day sitting outside the principal's office. I had an art teacher named Kim Bissett who was kind of a hippie, at least in the context of Catholic school, and she seemed to like me, and she was definitely my favorite teacher. One day I got called out of homeroom to talk to her. When I got to her room, she was crying. My heart sank. *Oh great,* I thought, *I finally have a teacher who likes me, the first one in my high school career, and now I'm making her cry.*

"You *won,*" she said. "You won…I hope you're not mad at me." I looked at her in total confusion. "I entered your art project into a state contest, and you won," she went on. Miss Bissett later told me about art therapy and I looked into it. For the first time, I considered college. That first step led me to my current profession.

I was with Miss Bissett one hour a week for one year, and she changed my life. You'll be doing the same with your students, no matter what kind of circumstances they face in their lives.

This being said, many teachers who work with this approach end up fielding questions from curious parents about their children's positively changed behaviors and attitudes. Teachers who use the approach begin to communicate differently with parents (more on this in the chapter on the Credit System, where you'll learn how to bring parents on board to mount a cooperative effort to foster their child's greatness in school *and* at home).

Notch It Up: Facing Off With a Really Tough Kid

When testing happens, it can be difficult to maintain your Stands. Challenging children know how to hurt others in ways that will get a big reaction, and your M.O. from here on is to refuse to energize in exactly the moment where you may feel more furious, hurt or afraid than you thought you could ever feel.

Remain emotionally neutral, at least on the outside. Breathe into the energy of whatever emotions are coming up for you. Use that energy as rocket fuel to lead you back into enhanced positive reflections. REFUSE to energize negativity; just reset any child who is breaking rules and stay focused on what's going right in the room. Remember and get very clear about the rules in your classroom; use those rules to find more positives to reflect upon. Welcome high-rollers back from resets with total clarity around what they are doing right and what they are not doing wrong.

Shifting Classroom and Peer Cultures With Resets

In the atmosphere of positivity created by time-in, the reset is highly effective, but inconsequential. Instead of the child experiencing shame in response to a consequence, he comes to trust that it is merely a pause in the path to seeing more of his greatness reflected back to him.

When time-in is authentic and consistently provided throughout the day, the culture of the classroom shifts. Children who feel nurtured do not compete for attention. They feel confident in sharing the spotlight because they perceive that there is no limit to the amount of emotional nutrition available to them.

A Nurtured Heart peer culture emerges. Students begin to speak to each other in the language of the approach. They begin to police each other and reset each other. Instead of egging each other on in negativity, they begin to energize one another's character and academic achievement. Often the toughest kids emerge as the leaders.

Phoenix, Arizona teacher and Advanced Trainer Amy Clarke Breitenbucher:

The Nurtured Heart Approach gives students the right to take ownership of their greatness. Students have a yearning to be in the company of classmates who recognize greatness in any moment. They also take ownership of their academics.

NHA builds classroom community, which in turn, allows for management of the classroom to be student-centered instead of teacher-directed. I heard one student tell another one, "You know, Thomas, you could have just punched me in the face right now for flicking food at you, and you didn't. I'm sorry for throwing food."

In this kind of peer culture, kids want to be at school. One parent wrote in a card that I received the last day of school, "I don't know what you did to my kid, but he wants to come to school now, even if he's throwing up."

Chapter Seven

Credit Systems For the Classroom

THE NURTURED HEART APPROACH can work beautifully without any credit system. If you do choose to use a credit system, however, it's important to make sure that it works *with* the approach, not against it. Those who already have a credit system in place may need to make a few adjustments in order to dovetail properly with the approach.

Again: a credit system is not necessary for successful implementation of this approach. If the three stands of the approach are maintained consistently, a positive social curriculum is quickly established in your classroom; children feel emotionally fed; and you'll face few discipline concerns, which may make a credit system unnecessary.

On the other hand, a Nurtured Heart credit system is a great way to get parents more involved in their child's academic life. It can help create a bridge of positivity and honest communication between home and school. As steady documentation of a child's successes in school is sent home to parents, everyone starts to speak the same Nurtured Heart language.

If your school policy dictates that each classroom must have an established discipline policy, a credit system could fill this requirement. If your school has already adopted its own discipline policy, a credit system can be used to support what is already in place, from the aspect of creating successes and time-in. A classroom credit system is also a great way to teach the rules and to create a sense of belonging and emotional safety. And a credit system is an excellent way to actively teach social-emotional curriculum in the classroom.

The Nurtured Heart Approach credit system can also:

- ✓ Support educators in consistently energizing students with a concrete measurement of successes.
- ✓ Be a good replacement for cost-involved systems or systems that involve dime-store toys or stickers; the relationship given through this credit system will prove far more valuable to students than dollar-store trinkets!
- ✓ Provide students with additional proactive connection instead of corrections for bad behavior.
- ✓ Provide educators with additional opportunity to reinforce target behaviors at the level of relationship.

- ✓ Be used to create and reinforce consistency among teams of teachers to create a Nurtured Heart-friendly policy across classrooms.
- ✓ Promote teamwork and cohesiveness among students as they work toward whole-class privileges.
- ✓ Provide a structure for handling conflict resolution and broken rules from a consistent, solution-based perspective.
- ✓ Provide additional support for target goals on IEP/540 plans.
- ✓ Provide a common language for students, teachers, administrators and parents.

A credit system for your classroom should reflect the value system and social curriculum you wish to support. We have included a few sample credit systems as a launching ground, but a vast amount of creativity is possible here as long as you stick with a few fundamentals.

The Nurtured Heart Approach Credit System

A Nurtured Heart Credit System is just another way to create super-energized relationship. This credit system should follow basic Nurtured Heart principles—the three Stands described throughout this book:

Stand 1: **Refuse to energize negativity.** Never take away points for bad behavior. That's what resets are for. **The credit system should *only* be used to energize good choices.** Use it to consistently reinforce good behavior. Points are accrued for all rules being followed; when a rule is broken, points cannot be spent until a reset is completed.

Stand 2: **Relentlessly energize the positive.** The sole purpose of a Nurtured Heart credit system is to *reinforce the flow of positive energy from educator to students.* Points flow in response to every *incremental* display of success. Provide ways to earn credits throughout the day and every day (not just on Fridays). Offer credits for values and qualities you wish to see and for rules not broken. Be *very* generous with points. You can't give too many points, just as you can't give too many recognitions of greatness. Give points for individual successes as well as classroom successes. Call students out on their successes throughout the day; refer to the points they've already earned to ensure that they know you are watching for greatness at every turn!

Avoid what I call the "garden hose" method of recognition: where you wait until the end of the day to energize, then try to make up for lost time by pouring it on. Think *drip irrigation:* feed them emotionally throughout the day, and they'll thrive.

The Nurtured Heart credit system consists of Ways to Earn and Ways to

Spend. When time-in is happening, points flow and spending is allowed (at the teacher's discretion). When rules are broken, points stop flowing until the reset is completed; then, the points flow again. Be careful not to remind or threaten a child who has broken a rule. Reset, and then give points at some later juncture for being on task, a leader, great learner, or whatever other quality you can find to energize on reentry to time-in.

If a child is about to break a rule, or you have an expectation that she's going to break a rule, it's still time-in. As long as that line hasn't been crossed, she can earn points.

***Never* use the credit system as a consequence.** If a student refuses a reset, spending of points or credits are "frozen" until the reset happens. Remain unattached to the child's choice to break the rule. Prove that negativity will no longer be rewarded with connected relationship.

Credit System Fundamentals

Start with "Ways to Earn" and "Ways to Spend." Ways to Earn can include everything from academic achievements (including simply staying on task, or even just staying in the chair) or to any choices to follow rules or display positive qualities or values.

Be generous with both points and behaviors that earn points. Give points/credits in increments of 100. This creates a sense of abundance in the realm of positivity, and it allows for partial credit.

What's true is that the number of credits a child has is an illusion. It's like going to one of those kid-friendly restaurants where $20 worth of tokens earns them a series of games, which in turn earns them a long string of tickets. They come running, utterly excited that they have 50,000 points. They return from the prize station with a plastic ring and some candy. If they really hit it big, they get their hands on a whoopie cushion!

Having a lot of points creates excitement and a sense of abundance, which translates to added potential for acting out abundant greatness. Let's say you offer 100 points for staying in one's chair, and Molly stays in her chair half the time. She can get 50 points instead of nothing.

Ways to Spend can include individual and group privileges. Think of privileges that allow students to help, support and energize one another privileges that build relationship, promote collaboration and teamwork, and encourage leadership. Avoid gimmicks and "treasure chest" trinkets! Here is an abbreviated list to get you started; on pages 125-126 of Glasser and Block's *Notching Up the Nurtured Heart Approach,* you'll find more complete lists of privileges.

Ways To Spend Points

Assisting a school staff member
Being a messenger
Choosing a sport, game, activity or story for the class
Computer time
Cruising the classroom offering appreciations to other students
Extra time with art materials
Good report home by phone or note
Having special reading time
Helping to decorate the classroom
Homework excuse passes
Lunch with the teacher
Recognition/appreciation note to the principal
Time to talk with a friend

Group Privileges

Chair switching time
Chalkboard doodle time
Face making time
Game time
Group appreciation fest
Group reading time
Noisemaking time
Pencil tapping time
Recognition/appreciation note to principal from entire class
Quiet art time

Ways to spend can be decided by the teacher or team. Students buy in more readily if their feedback and ideas are considered. One teacher I worked with had "iPod Fridays," where her high school students were allowed to listen to music while doing class work.

To build leadership and independence, offer a Junior Peacefinder, Greatness Grabber or Greatness Guide privilege, which allows students to wander the classroom or lunchroom wearing a special hat, button or lanyard. Their job: to energize fellow classmates who are in the act of creating greatness. This creates a new energetic trajectory in the classroom: a culture that, at its center, is about what is going well. It also makes learning and appropriate interactions the prize.

One teacher challenged her class to individually complete and record 100 random acts of kindness as a part of their writing curriculum. At another school, students earn "Lunch with the Dean" as a way of creating positive relationships with the vice principal and discipline dean. "Lunch and Literature" is another privilege in which students get to have lunch in the classroom with their teacher and discuss their favorite books.

Who Should Be On a Credit System?

Many teachers resist putting the whole classroom on a credit system because they think it will be more work. This is understandable, because teachers are required to track and document astounding amounts of information. In one classroom, I watched a teacher spend an entire day documenting information, leaving her no time to teach! She told me, "So many children in my class have IEPs...I have to track and document many times each hour to be in compliance." She barely had time to teach the lesson due to all the additional paperwork.

Yes, a credit system is a commitment, and it takes time to create on the front end. Once in place, though, it becomes a part of what you do as a teacher. The whole point is to create inner wealth, and the whole point of inner wealth is to inspire students to be more self-sufficient. Having them keep track of their own successes is a way to foster independence. In the end, this will *lighten* your work load.

If you have a credit system in place, it is our recommendation that all students be on it. Some students' credit systems will require more detail than others (due to IEPs or 504 plans); some teachers use a spreadsheet to keep track when not every student is on the same credit system. Having a separate credit sheet folder for each child allows for confidentiality and organization for parent-teacher conferences.

If you have children with IEPs or 504 plans, their goals can be incorporated into their credit systems. This is a great way for teachers to demonstrate that they are actively targeting specific behaviors. Also, it keeps the student focused on target behaviors and provides a concrete way for him to track his success.

Notching it Up!

Make some decisions about your credit system using the blank form on the next page, even if you aren't sure whether you will use one.

Include individual and group privileges.

And finally, brainstorm ways to keep track of points. Teachers' creativity really shines here! Students can be held responsible for tracking their own points, or you can use tokens, chips, play money, checking registers or worksheets.

Ways to Earn	Points	Ways to Spend	Points

(If you run out of space here, there's another page at the very back of the book where you can continue to brainstorm Ways to Earn and Ways to Spend.)

Explaining The Credit System to Your Students

Ideally, you'll roll out the credit system at the beginning of your year together. It can come later and still be successful, but the beginning of the year is a natural starting point.

Explain the credit system to children with the purpose of engaging them in the classroom culture. This is the perfect time to explain your rules, boundaries, and expectations in terms of rules NOT broken and the points that they'll earn for not breaking those rules. This is a great path for self-discovery for students: it illustrates that the rules are their friends. And it's an exciting way to apply mathemetics in the classroom!

For example:

"One of the ways to earn is by not breaking any of the posted rules. For each day you are successful, you will earn 100 credits."

"When you act with integrity, demonstrate teamwork, and show initiative, you will earn 300 credits."

It is also a time for students to see *how* they will get your energy and attention. Discussing this through the credit system amounts to making a pact with them about how you will treat them, how you expect to be treated, and what you will not tolerate. This process builds trust that supports the whole implementation of the approach.

Welcome opportunities to demonstrate how you will handle a toe on the line. During this discussion you will surely have a few in the mix that will need to test your congruency meter. This is the perfect time to introduce the reset and to immediately welcome back and restore the relationship. When you are fearless and clear in your intention and purpose, they learn what kind of toy you'll be from day one!

As discussed earlier, you will create more buy-in from your students if, after explaining the system, you initiate a discussion about ways they might earn and spend points. You get final say in what ends up on the list, but children feel more invested when they have a voice—especially older children.

Lastly, involve parents in the process. Send a letter home explaining your new discipline policy. Explain to parents that sometimes, children will earn points at school for choices or behaviors at home. At Parent Night, offer a mini-introduction to the approach for parents of your students. When parent workshops are offered to bridge the gap between home and school, the approach is often much more effective. They get more parent involvement, greater homework compliance, and less conflict between parents and school.

For a comprehensive view of what a parent workshop would look like, refer to the *Nurtured Heart Approach Workbook for Parents*[1] as your guide.

---

1. JoAnne Bowdidge, Lisa Bravo, and Howard Glasser, *Transforming the Difficult Child Workbook: An Interactive Guide to the Nurtured Heart Approach for Parents, Teachers, Practitioners and All Other Caregivers,* Nurtured Heart Publications, Tucson, AZ: 2008.

Chapter Eight

Spreading the Word in School and to Parents

The AZELLA exam measures English comprehension. Students K-12 in Arizona are mandated to take this test. Students who cannot pass this exam are required to be separated from the general school population until they are able to pass it.

Rhett Etherton's Phoenix, Arizona 6th-8th grade classroom of was comprised of 25 students, mostly boys, who were unable to pass the AZELLA exam. A majority of these students also had a history of disciplinary issues. Rhett's students came from the surrounding poor, crime-ridden community. Their attendance at school was unstable and their academic performance poor. Many were known throughout the school as troublemakers.

Rhett had been trained in the Nurtured Heart Approach for some time at that point. He called me after he'd been assigned this group of students for the following year. After he explained the demographics to me, I asked him, "How do you feel about this kind of challenge?" After a brief silence he answered, "Bring it on! There is no kid out there that I can't handle. I'm honored to be chosen…and I know those kids will never be the same!"

For the next year, Rhett carried out his mission to turn these students around. He nurtured and disciplined them. Some of his colleagues laughed at him; they didn't believe the approach would work, especially with these kids. Rhett persevered. He refused to energize the negativity of his coworkers or that of his students. He was known as a strict teacher among the student body, yet everyone wanted to be in his class.

Rhett created a system of support among his peers and a daily practice of reinforcing himself in greatness. He started a "greatness group" that met in the early morning at the beginning of each week at a local coffee shop. The purpose: to energize each other. The first meeting consisted of just Rhett and one other person; soon, the numbers rose past 20, and included the school's principal and its janitor.

That year, so many students tested out of his classroom that he no longer had enough students. He was reassigned to teaching third grade. In 2010, Rhett received an Innovative Teacher of the Year award. He has become the Nurtured Heart Approach expert in the school and now provides training to his peers.

Rhett's story is extraordinary to the layperson. Really, how could creating relationship change so much in a classroom or school? How many teachers will joyfully take on the toughest students? In our world, Rhett is not an aberration. But when I first met him, he was contemplating leaving teaching altogether.

Back then, he shared with me that he was exhausted each day with the negative climate in which he worked, and with trying to discipline and teach students who did not want to be there. When he began to use the approach in his classroom, he noticed he felt more alive and energized. As his students began to respond academically and behaviorally, he was inspired to begin a daily regimen of self-care that included meditation, yoga, and healthy nutrition.

The students in Rhett's classroom will likely always come from poverty and difficult circumstances. He has no control over that. He *does* have the capacity and skill to see and honor each student in a way that is irrefutable. This purity and intensity of relationship is the core of the approach.

We train thousands of teachers each year. At this writing, teachers, administrators, and districts are implementing the Nurtured Heart Approach in individual classrooms around the country and around the world. Only a handful work in a school or a school system where implementation is system-wide. This is unfortunate, because in those schools and school systems, the results are even better.

Typically, we see system-wide implementation when schools are "poorly performing" or their academic proficiencies are being questioned. People are far more motivated to change when their backs are against the wall. In schools that aren't in crisis, the Nurtured Heart movement may catch on more slowly. If your school has big fires to put out, chances are better that other educators will be open to learning and applying the approach.

Let's get you prepared to explain the approach to anyone who asks.

Notching it Up!

Near the end of our week-long Advanced Trainings, Howard and I often ask participants to create a "one-minute pitch" that could be used to introduce others to the approach. Take a moment now to craft your own one-minute pitch for the inevitable moment when fellow teachers, administrators or parents ask what you're doing differently in your classroom: for fellow teachers; for parents of your students; and for administrators.

Inspiration to Whole-School Implementation

If you are the "Lone Ranger" in your school, you may feel frustrated as students enjoy the approach's benefits only in your classroom, while in the rest of the school, things are the way they've always been. Once you've succeeded in flipping upside-down energy right-side up, you may begin to see even more clearly how upside-down the energy is just outside your classroom doors.

You may have concerns that this undermines all your heartfelt work in changing classroom culture and cultivating greatness. You may also begin to notice how upside-down energy pervades interactions between coworkers and the way your school is run.

Once you recognize the power of the Nurtured Heart Approach in shifting the culture of your classroom, you will probably want to promote and support its use by other teachers in your school. You may even want to introduce the idea of full-school implementation to administrators.

Top-down implementation where administrators are on board and help bring teachers on board is most smooth, effective and efficient. This way, a non-punitive Nurtured Heart structure can be implemented most smoothly school-wide. Administrators have the power to send key people to be trained, which spares the school the effort and expense of bringing in outside trainers. The approach can then be built into the culture of the school.

Many Nurtured Heart teachers have been swimming upstream for a long time. Their principals may be supportive insofar as they see Nurtured Heart only as a mode of classroom management, but they may not be interested in promoting the approach's spread into other classrooms or implementing it from the top down. Even if they don't respond in kind, you will experience rewards if you are able to bring the approach into relationships with coworkers and bosses.

Know that people feel instinctively resistant in the face of change. Even when it starts with a single teacher, students' inner wealth grows. They learn to carry the energy of greatness with them wherever they go; they develop reserves. They'll also learn to carry the energy of the un-energized reset into other classrooms. Consequences will no longer feel like rewards in your classroom, and they'll take that with them.

The Greatness of Amy Sward

Amy is the principal of the North Education Center in Intermediate District 287 near Minneapolis, Minnesota. Students with serious behavioral issues are referred from nearby districts, as well as from other districts whose special education strategies haven't met the complex needs of these students. Amy has spent 25 years working with students with special needs; discovering the Nurtured Heart Approach revolutionized her work with these kids.

The students at my school have more than special needs: they have intense needs coupled with significant behaviors. These are the students who get me in touch with my energy, my humility, my intensity, my heart. I believe these students wake up every morning planning to have a great day, to demonstrate their greatness…and somewhere, things take a turn. Students who possess the intense energy that leads to a referral to a Setting IV program have typically experienced life differently. Often, our students have seen and done things in their short lives that many of us will not experience in a lifetime.

Schools work with students who can't read by teaching them the strategies they need to read. When a student struggles in math, they are taught strategies to improve their math skills. However, when a student struggles to behave, they are often medicated, removed from the classroom, or told they will not be able to participate in something important to them. We have to teach these students to manage their intensity so they can more fully participate in all aspects of life.

Believing that all children are born to be great, I know that punishment is not what changes behavior. No consequence, no matter how drastic, is enough to impact these young people on a long-term basis. We need to work differently with these children; we need to embrace their intensity. These students are like a bucket with a small hole in the bottom: The student needs to plug that hole before they can fill their bucket. How do we support students in plugging the hole? We let them know that they are in control of their energy and of their futures. When students recognize that they have what they need to manage whatever comes at them, they begin plugging the hole and are better able to learn.

After attending the week-long Nurtured Heart Approach Advanced Training in 2009, my social-emotional learning coordinator, Katherine Utter, and I returned determined to implement the approach in classrooms and programs, and eventually in the entire building. We trained and encouraged staff to practice recognizing students. Nothing fancy: we all just practiced seeing students through the lens of greatness and telling the students what was seen. I saw my job as doing the same for staff. The following year, we fully implemented the approach for our EBD (emotional-behavioral disorder) programs while piloting the approach in our autism classrooms. We offered cohorts, mini trainings, classes, videotaping, and more.

The changes we saw were beyond what we had hoped. Students were spending more time in their classrooms; their listening comprehension skills were exploding, increasing 1.5 years over the course of the year; the use of a time-out room diminished; we went from a full-time School Resource Officer to part-time. Eventually, the room utilized for time-outs was repurposed into a classroom. We had a setting IV program without a time-out room! Staff made comments about running out of curriculum because they could teach more to their students. We noticed students recognizing each other's greatness and the greatness of their staff. Behavioral incidents were decreasing and problems related to intensity decreased as well. Parents were seeing improvements at home and wanted information on the approach.

As of 2011, implementation was building-wide, regardless of the educational label attached to the student. We implement with all. Who doesn't need recognition of their greatness? We are setting clearer limits, recognizing with greater clarity, and refusing to give energy to all things negative. We make mistakes and we move on.

As the administrators of this amazing staff, John Fry, Assistant Principal, and I have changed our roles. We continue recognizing the greatness in our staff. We find ourselves giving permission to those in the classrooms to recognize what is going well during a difficult altercation. We find ourselves giving staff permission to ask for help, to struggle with clarity and to choose recognizing greatness in times of what appears to be chaos. The Nurtured Heart Approach has offered a path to recognizing the heart and greatness of every student in every situation. As a team we choose this path every day. It's as if our lives depend on it…but really, it's our students' lives that depend on it!

The Nurtured Heart Workplace

A few years ago, while working on the first Nurtured Heart Approach workbook with Howard Glasser and JoAnne Bowdidge, I worked in a hospital emergency room doing psychiatric and behavioral health assessments. It was a toxic environment, and the irony was obvious: even as I wrote this workbook on nurturing others' hearts, I spent much of the day writing suicide and rape assessments.

Even worse was the toxicity I sensed among my coworkers. They were chin-deep in negativity and sinking fast. To stay sane, I took it upon myself to find six things that were going well in each day. I wanted to find a way to share this with others, but knew that my coworkers would not be able to hear or trust positive messages, at least not at first. So I started writing anonymous notes to energize others.

As my notes were discovered, I overheard people asking, "Who's doing this?" At first, they thought it was our boss. They were distrustful. But when I stopped writing the notes, people complained about not getting them anymore! They had begun to look for them and share them with each other. Just that one small step changed the culture of that stressful place.

Notching it Up!

Use the space below to jot a few notes about the greatness of a colleague. Who else would you like to energize? What gifts and qualities do you want to call them out on?

As you awaken to the joy and wisdom of your students and fully embrace your gifts and talents as a teacher, you will feel more energized. As you create a Nurtured Heart culture in the classroom and by being who you are, you'll find yourself less willing to speak about the atrocities of the day: to gossip, complain, resist or attack, or to respond to others defensively. It will affect your interactions in the classroom, the teacher's lounge, at staff meetings, and in your exchanges with other teachers and parents.

Notching it Up!

Brainstorm some ideas about how to create a 'greatness culture' among your colleagues: educators, administrators, support staff.

____

____

____

____

____

____

Working With Resistance

Let's face it: most people, educators included, find it challenging to consistently tap into their inner wisdom and their commitment to live fully in greatness. Know in advance that as you grow the greatness and inner wealth of your students, you'll be faced with comparable challenges and opportunities along the trajectory of your own growth.

If you are met with resistance as you try to bring the Nurtured Heart Approach to a system, respond in exactly the same way we suggest when resistance arises in students: *embrace it!* Resistance is just energy. It will shift in the direction of change. Complacency and apathy are bigger obstacles than resistance.

Ask your fellow teachers and administrators: *What is your vision as an educator? Does your vision for your school involve teaching kids to love and believe in themselves, be kind and helpful to others, and to love learning?* Let them know that as a universal social curriculum, the Nurtured Heart Approach is aligned with every aspect of this vision.

Schools that have adopted the Nurtured Heart Approach school-wide are, at this writing, a small percentage of all schools in existence. Many schools already have an allegiance to more traditional forms of discipline. They may be committed to other methods in which they have invested significant time and financial resources.

Although designed to be used on its own, the Nurtured Heart Approach can help other programs flourish at greater levels. An organic progression usually occurs over the years to yield the mixture that fulfills the needs of students and adults alike.

Is the Nurtured Heart Approach Stand-Alone... or Can It Work With Other Programs?

When districts have invested money and time in another approach, they are (understandably) reluctant to start over with the Nurtured Heart Approach. As a result, we've had to gain some level of flexibility in integrating our method with other approaches in the school setting.

At this writing, this approach is in its infancy in educational settings. It has been necessary for trainers and teachers who use the approach to work within the framework of other programs when they have been designated by school districts, often at considerable cost.

Teacher Amy Clarke Breitenbucher was asked to teach one very popular positive behavioral approach to student teachers at Arizona State University. After becoming an Advanced Trainer in the Nurtured Heart Approach, she instead chose to teach the Nurtured Heart Approach. When I asked her how she feels these approaches can work together in the school setting, she answered:

The first thing most approaches want teachers to find out in the wake of misbehavior is the "why." This is what teachers are told to focus on when faced with a difficult child. But understanding why *the child behaves in a certain way doesn't change anything. Yes, Johnny's dad was shot in a gang fight last year, his mother has just been arrested for being undocumented and his 13-year-old sister is pregnant and has to share a room with him, and soon he'll be sleeping on the couch. And yes, it's helpful for the teacher to have some knowledge of a student's struggles, but in the Nurtured Heart Approach, those struggles do not change our expectations of Johnny... To fail to hold Johnny to the same academic and behavioral expectations as his peers insults and disservices him. If we intend to hold him to the same expectations, does the "why" really matter?*

Advanced Trainer Bud Weiss, who has taught the same behavioral approach in schools, shared more about how the NHA can clash with more traditional approaches:

Teachers themselves are not empowered to deal with difficult children in other approaches. A team is assigned and trained especially to handle difficult kids, and if that team is unsuccessful, the child is promoted to a higher level of special education, with a different team of teachers. These children are channeled further and further from the mainstream, creating more and more expense. Isolating and promoting troubled children feeds negative patterns and works at odds with the Nurtured Heart Approach.

Although using the Nurtured Heart Approach with other approaches can present challenges like these, it does maximize relationship building in any context. When combined with other methods, this approach creates more efficient classroom engagement and improves the effectiveness of other programs. Teachers have called it "Miracle-Grow" for this very reason. Research is underway to measure this amplifying effect.

The Special Ed Classroom and IEPs/504s

Children who are difficult or intense are often mislabeled with learning disorders and behavioral disorders. These children show up in school with jam-packed negative portfolios. Students in Special Education programs often don't believe they can be successful. They lack confidence and need more help from adults around them. They struggle with anxiety and end up in state of arousal. Sitting still becomes almost impossible for them. (Try sitting still when *you're* in a state of anxious arousal!) When schools respond to their academic problems by lowering expectations and moving them to lower class levels, their portfolios are further loaded with negative ideas about their own brilliance. But when educators nurture these students' greatness, their anxiety is diminished. Their academic problems can more easily be solved.

IEPs are created by schools for children who meet criteria for learning disability. 504 plans are designed to support children with disabilities in having equal access to federally funded education programs. A child with a physical disability, chronic illness or psychiatric diagnosis may need a 504 plan. While a 504 is more about creating a "level playing field" so that students with disabilities have opportunities on a par with other students, an IEP is about creating an educational plan.

Parents see IEPs/504 plans as a way to provide advocacy for their child's educations. Schools see them as cumbersome requirements that can't always be fulfilled to everyone's satisfaction. Although intended to provide a bridge, they often create division. But because of the legal requirements of special education, they may be needed in your classroom.

Children diagnosed with ADHD are often given the designation "Emotionally/Behaviorally Disabled" (EBD) for IEP purposes. The EBD child is a great candidate for a Nurtured Heart-friendly IEP. Integrate Nurtured Heart language and positive reflections on the child's successes. This way, you can maintain the level of measurability that's needed to keep accurate track of the child's progress without shifting into negativity. For example: Instead of saying, "Mary will not show aggression 80 percent of the time," say, "Mary will be assertive and articulate in saying what she needs 80 percent of the time." Make it a *strength-based* IEP rather than a liability-based IEP.

On many occasions, I have sat in IEP review meetings at the request of the parents. The atmosphere is often contentious; the family has its own ideas about what the child needs to achieve academic success, and these do not always match what the school is able to accommodate. In actuality, both parties want the same thing: for the child to be successful and happy. Reflect this common goal by using Nurtured Heart language in these meetings whenever possible. When the language and skill set of the Nurtured Heart Approach are implemented within the context of the IEP meeting, different levels of purpose and intention come forth. Everyone feels heard, appreciated and understood.

In Nurtured Heart schools, far fewer requests for IEP evaluation are generated. Before implementing the approach, about 15 percent of students at Tolson Elementary in Tucson had IEPs; a few years later, that number had fallen to only one percent.

Introducing the Nurtured Heart Approach to Parents

The most common story told by a parent who discovers this approach is a variation on the theme of my story, as told earlier in this book: Overwhelmed by the demands of an intense child, they seek a way to better relate to and support that child.

On the other hand, teachers of intense children need to use care in introducing the approach to the parents of these children. If I'm a parent of an intense child and someone puts a Nurtured Heart book in my hands while I'm at an IEP meeting or at a meeting with the principal (about problems), I just might bite because I'm so frustrated and discouraged and want some help or, for that same reason, I might resist, because I'm so tired of everyone giving me parenting advice because they think it's my fault that my child is difficult.

The way around this is to introduce the approach to parents *in a positive context*, telling the detailed truth about the strengths of the child before introducing the knowledge you'd like them to receive. "Mrs. Smith, I wanted to let you know how much I enjoy having Ben in my class. He is so resourceful and helpful, and he's making great progress in his level of effort with academics. I wanted to share with you some things I've learned that I believe have helped Ben to live out his greatness in the classroom."

A form can be created to communicate with parents about a difficult student's greatness. Glasser and Block's *Notching Up the Nurtured Heart Approach* contains a sample form on page 128.

Notching it Up!

Think of a particular difficult child in your classroom. How would you energize him or her directly? Then, consider how you might introduce the approach to his or her parent. Write what you might say in the space below.

If you were to create a form that could be sent home to acknowledge a student's greatness to his or her parents, what would that look like?

Many parents of intense children feel they have had to fight the school system to advocate for the children. They may be ready for a battle any time you want to talk with them about their child. In other words: parents of intense children can be just as difficult as their children! As a trainer, I still have to shake off my own "heebie-jeebies" when asked to facilitate training in a school setting where I may face angry, oppositional parents.

Expect parents to be skeptical of you and your motives at first. Many of these parents are stuck in a punitive framework, and mightily resist any other approach. These parents know their child is a handful, and they know how frustrating it can be.

Although I *loved* Christopher, my once-difficult child, I still found him impossible at times. Still, my mama bear would come out when I realized that his teacher, the person with whom Christopher had to spend all day, every weekday, might not even like him. I worried that he might be mistreated or treated unfairly. If his teachers had made a habit of coming to me to talk about my child's strengths instead of his weaknesses, my ready-for-a-fight state would quickly have dissolved into gratitude and a desire to work with my son's teacher to create a better experience for everyone. Now, I have the opportunity to help create this kind of safety for parents and their children. So do you.

Chapter Nine

Experiential Exercises For Educators

The man who believes he can and the man who believes he cannot are always right.

—Confucius

When teachers begin to learn this approach, they sometimes say they don't have time for for it in their busy school days. And this seems like a sensible concern, as long as they consider it an "add-on" to everything they already do, including teaching academics and dealing with administrative and bureaucratic details.

Most social-emotional programs require additional curriculum-based lessons, specialized lesson planning, and tracking to substantiate implementation. This adds a significant amount of time and busy work for teachers. The Nurtured Heart Approach is implemented in a fundamentally different way. It isn't meant to be an "on the shelf" curriculum, but a part of the classroom culture and of your natural classroom flow. It clearly addresses the social and emotional needs of the students, which creates space for academics to soar!

Given this truth, the time factor isn't an impediment. Think of this approach as something to be integrated into every aspect of the life of your classroom, not as something to be done or taught outside of academics. Regard it as scaffolding that supports the classroom and everything that goes on within it.

This approach is a hands-on way to teach interpersonal and intrapersonal social-emotional skills. It's visceral and experiential, not cognitive or cerebral. Consider it the background culture in which you conduct the business of your classroom, where the narrative of the classroom is transformed into a conversation about noticing and recognizing greatness in one another.

Weave the approach into your interactions with students throughout the day. Instead of giving them a lecture about responsibility, confront them *in the moment* that they are being responsible. Create firsthand experiences that generate a cumulative experience of success (both academic and social). Commit to integrating recognitions and celebrations of greatness into every aspect of classroom life.

Once educators really *get* this approach, they begin to generate tools for their classrooms that reflect their own unique ways of relating with students. Several of these tools and techniques for actualizing Nurtured Heart concepts in classrooms are described in this chapter. Use these experiential pieces as-is, or use them as a springboard for your own creative versions; the journaling boxes will give you opportunities to consider experiential applications of your own.

Experiential exercises assist in defining classroom culture, creating success, and teaching children about rules and limits. A crucial thread is the pure intention of creating, building, and supporting inner wealth as a way of defining classroom culture. Exercises like these help weave this thread through your daily routine, weaving a substantial fabric that is the backdrop for all academic success.

Although most of these activities can work with children of any age, some are more appropriate for certain age groups or developmental stages. Let's start out with a few notions about Nurtured Heart activities appropriate for different age ranges.

Preschoolers

Preschool-aged children learn experientially, kinesthetically and in the moment. They tend to be wide open to seeing their own greatness and the greatness of others. Not surprisingly, they respond well to the immediacy of the Nurtured Heart Approach. Educators can 'super-energize' preschoolers' experiences of success through energizing recognitions. Cumulative moments of success accrue quickly and have big impact with children in this age range, across all demographics.

Preschoolers respond particularly well to Active Recognitions, where the adult simply describes what she sees as though she were describing it to a blind person. A child doing an art project hears, "I see you're putting lines of purple next to lines of pink. Some of the lines are dark and thick because you're pressing hard on your crayon, and others are lighter and thinner," and this translates to: *I see you. You are not invisible! You are important. You are loved. Adults around you will give you connected, energized relationship just for being exactly who you are and expressing that in what you do.*

Elementary Schoolers (K–6th)

Elementary schoolers are still quite malleable; they are still defining their roles in the game of life, and are highly impressionable and resilient. They adapt well when upside-down energy is flipped right side up. Elementary-aged "high rollers" have greater potential to move readily out of negative behavior into patterns of leadership and positive peer culture than those who aren't exposed to this approach until middle or high school. Intervention at this developmental juncture reaps great success.

Middle Schoolers (6th/7th-8th/9th)

If you are the parent or teacher of a middle schooler, you already know what a potentially tumultuous time this is for "tweeners." The developmental stage between childhood and adolescence is the stage where young people are most likely to succumb to peer pressure. According to research by Florida State University sociology professors John Taylor and Donald Lloyd and University of Miami professor emeritus George Warheit, low self-esteem and peer approval of drug use at age 11 predicts drug dependency at age 20. Children with very low self-esteem, which the researchers termed "self-derogation," were 1.6 times more likely to meet the criteria for drug dependence nine years later than other children. In another study, researchers in Indianapolis, Indiana found that 40 percent of seventh- to ninth-grade girls who scored low on a test of self-esteem at the start of seventh grade had lost their virginity by ninth grade. Only 18 percent of girls with the highest scores had become sexually active by that time.

The middle-school child is in the process of defining who he is to his peer group. When teachers tilt the playing field in the direction of greatness, middle-school students willingly play along; this greatly reduces the complexities of poor peer influence and all but eliminates bullying. The intense middle-schooler may have already formed the impression that he gets incredible returns from both peers and adults through acting out. This is the student who can turn your classroom upside down in seconds and has a knack for getting all the other students to follow suit.

From an energetic perspective, if you see this student as a strong leader, you can create a different 'channel' for that middle-schooler student to use his skills as a leader in a positive way. The trick is to convince him and fellow students that there is *so* much more energetic connection available in response to moments and instances of integrity, responsibility, respectfulness, discipline, and cooperation.

High Schoolers (9th/10th-12th)

When I travel around the country giving workshops and trainings, I typically see only a handful of teachers coming from a high school setting. Most are Special Education teachers or school counselors. I hold a special place in my heart for those of you who still see the importance of nurturing the hearts of children at the high school level. I do not have to tell you that this age group is especially challenging to reach.

However, I promise: it's *not too late!* I've had the pleasure of working with some of the toughest teens on our planet through my work in the juvenile justice system. As their court-ordered therapist, I had the chance to "cut my teeth" with some of the toughest, most resistant teens around. What I found to be true among *all* of them is that they had built their lives and self-images on being adversarial. They were excellent at getting others to follow them and skilled at reading energy. The energy of fear was one that they all knew well and they knew how to take full advantage of it. They were keenly aware of their personal power and how to use it to influence those around them, and this formed the basis of their self-concept and beliefs about how to be successful in their lives.

What I learned early on is how to meet their energy, match it, and use the tools of the approach to channel this energy into the place of fearless leadership, personal integrity, and vast inner wealth. I learned that ALL children, no matter the age or circumstance, have a strong desire to be powerful, wise, responsible, and influential. When they are able to see that they can embrace their intensity *and* still be in charge in an ever more powerful way, they no longer need the imbalanced energy of negative interactions. With this mindset and the relentless application of the Nurtured Heart Approach, I've seen many "worst" teens transformed into young men and women who are all about greatness!

Creating Nurtured Heart Classrooms

Most teachers fill their walls with visually appealing materials meant to encourage learning. Nurtured Heart can provide a framework and model that will enable you to be purposeful and intentional about how you create classroom space. Let your 'wall stuff' (bulletin boards and visual aids) support the recognition of greatness and your three Stands. A few examples:

- ✓ A teacher in New Jersey places half-teacups on the wall for each student. Every time she accuses a student of perserverance, working hard, working well with others, or demonstrating some other quality of greatness, she places a sugar cube in the student's teacup and announces the quality to the child: "Lilly, I want to give you some sugar right now because you are showing great leadership in the way you requested that your group get back on topic."

✓ Create portfolios for each child, each labeled with a photograph and displayed on the wall. Each child can write down his or her experiences of greatness and success to slide into the portfolio. Its contents can then be shared at parent-teacher conferences or appointed times when educators connect with students. Students can also have designated times to share their portfolios with each other.

✓ In one preschool classroom, a teacher created a Juicy Word Wall where she glued oranges made from construction paper, each with a word she considered descriptive of students' greatness. Children got extra accolades when they used words from the wall.

✓ Traditionally, behavior charts used at Rancho Romero Elementary in northern California have said, "How Am I Doing Today?" across the top, with student numbers below and a pocket for cards for each student. Students would start out each day with a green card; also in the pockets were yellow and red cards. Poor choices would mean turning the green card to yellow or even to red. A third-grade teacher at Rancho Romero decided, after learning about the Nurtured Heart Approach, to transform this punitive card system into a compliments chart. Gone are the red, yellow and green cards; in their place are spaces for compliments, written on cards by fellow students and slipped into the appropriate numbered pocket.

In the Nurtured Heart classroom, the "How Am I Doing" wall with red, yellow and green cards can become...

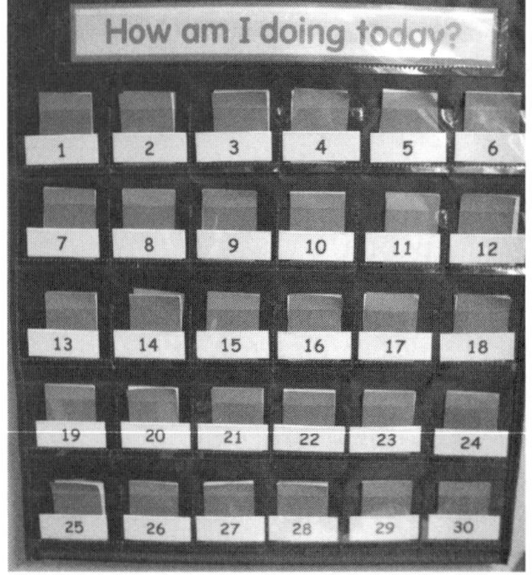

*...the **Compliments Wall**!*

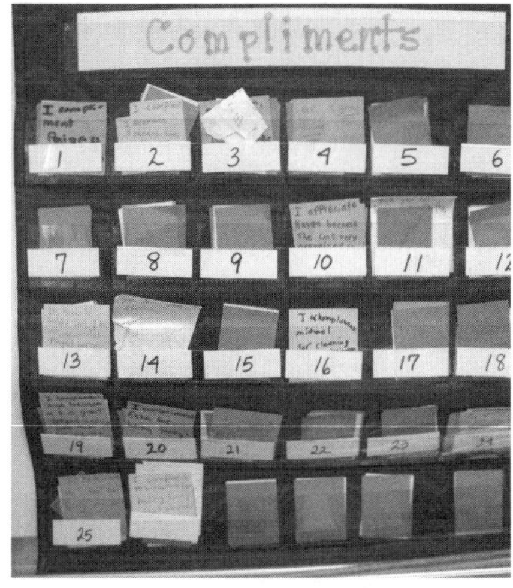

✓ Cooley Middle School special education teacher Celeste Elsey created "Greatness Graffiti," a system where students could write about one another's greatness where all could see it. A fourth-grade teacher at Rancho Romero adapted Celeste's idea. Students had previously worked on energizing each other in class. Each student drew a classmate's name out of a cup and used sentence stems to create energizing statements about that classmate. The statements were posted for parents to read during Back to School Night.

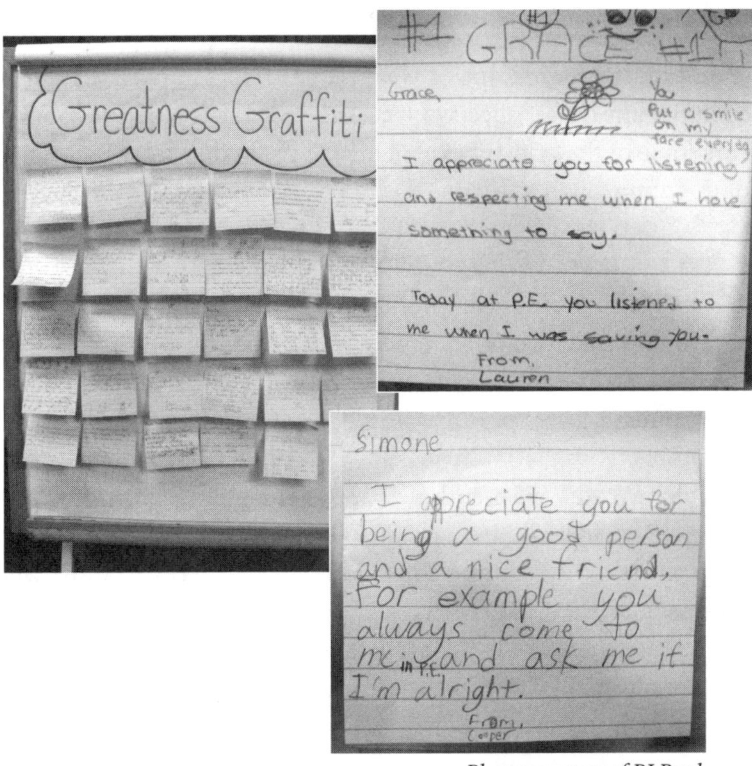

Photos courtesy of BJ Byrd, P.E. teacher at Rancho Romero Elementary

Notching it Up!

Brainstorm a few of your own ideas for changing the 'hardscape' of your classroom to integrate Nurtured Heart concepts and practice.

Aside from the hardscape of your classroom, the approach can be integrated into many other aspects of teaching and creation of classroom culture. Here are some of the brilliant experiential tools used by teachers who are masters of this approach.

Teaching Language With the Nurtured Heart Approach

This approach enables educators to teach descriptive words in context to teach words like *collaborative, rational, courageous,* or *inquisitive* in a way that's congruent with tone and intention. When we 'catch' them embodying these qualities, students learn these words in a deep way and can easily use them regarding others.

The Juicy Word Wall mentioned above is a good exercise for preschool classrooms. For older children, try introducing Challenge Words about qualities of greatness. Offer extra credit throughout the week to those who learn greatness language.

Try adding qualities of greatness to the weekly spelling or vocabulary list as bonus words to spell or use in a sentence, then ring a bell every time a child uses these words in the classroom.

Notching it Up!

Come up with another way in which language can be taught to your students through the techniques/intentions of the Nurtured Heart Approach.

Greatness Guidelines

This is a way to talk about classroom rules in context of the Nurtured Heart Approach. It's a variation on the theme of Proactive Recognition. Work with students on describing themselves following the rules and the ways in which this reflects their greatness.

"I show my greatness when I take turns."

"I show how great I am when I help others."

"I show my greatness by not interrupting or being disruptive."

Using the word *greatness* helps them understand the expectation.

Notching it Up!

Consider some other ways you might integrate Proactive Recognition into classroom activities.

____

____

____

____

____

____

Greatness Detectives

At the beginning of class, San Francisco Bay area elementary-school physical education teacher BJ Byrd will often have students choose a partner. Their job during the rest of class is to be "greatness detectives" to be on the lookout for ways in which their partners show their greatness. While the group stretches at the end of class, BJ has students stand next to their partners and energize them for their greatness: "I energize you for..." or "I accuse you of... Students are encouraged to be as specific as possible. BJ says, "An additional benefit of this exercise is that students fight over who s going to energize me!"

Greatness Lectures

One of Rhett Etherton's brilliant classroom methods is to deliver "greatness lectures":

One of the main reasons that students are called up to the teacher's desk is being in trouble. Students almost wince when they hear their name called by the teacher, knowing that they will probably get a long lecture on what they did wrong and why it was so wrong. In my classroom, I give Greatness Lectures. Between lessons, I'll say a student's name in a serious way and tell him or her to come to my desk. Then, I'll start lecturing the student about the greatness he or she showed during the past lesson.

One day I called up a student named Christian, who had recently moved to Arizona from Mexico. Learning a new language can bring up anxiety and fear, so I wanted to make sure he knew how great he was being. Speaking slowly and using hand gestures, I energized him for passing his quiz that day. I accused him of being resourceful and then asked him to tell me how he was being resourceful. "I asked a friend to help me understand the English," he said. I told him, "That's what great students do." I gave him a high-five and told him he could go back to his seats. While I'm not sure if he understood every word I was saying, I knew that he felt my energy and knew he was showing greatness.

Notching it Up!

Write a 'greatness lecture' for someone in your life: a student, a coworker, a spouse, one of your children, or even yourself.

'Heart Attack' Another Class

Cut hearts out of paper. Have students write down what they notice about teachers or students in other classrooms. (If they are too young to write, teachers can write these items on the hearts for them.) From time to time, surprise the other class by putting hearts all over the classroom.

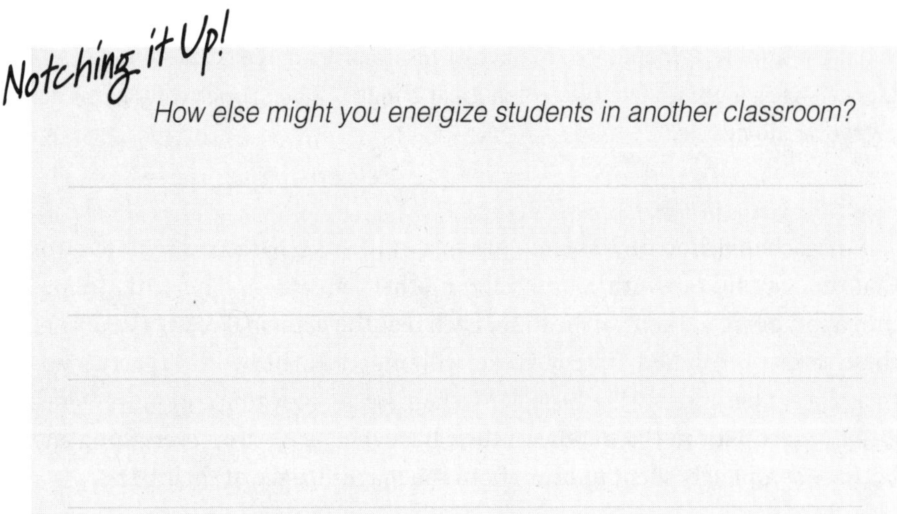

Greatness Goggles

Make 'greatness goggles' and decorate them. Students can be chosen to stand up, don the goggles and talk specifically and irrefutably about others' greatness in the classroom. If you have a credit system in place, you can also offer this as a privilege that can be purchased with points. In place of goggles, teachers might opt for a lanyard with a Greatness Grabber badge, a hat, a smock, a crown or a scepter. For older children, a clipboard or funny sunglasses might be a better choice.

Mystery Student

This activity helps build positive peer culture. It's a good way to pull in outlier kids who tend to get picked on. Start by writing each student's name on something that can be picked out of a can, such as tongue depressors or craft sticks, and ceremoniously choose a student each morning. Announce who has been picked: "The mystery student of the morning is Sam." Identify what he's doing right. "I've picked his stick out and look, he's on track with the assignment, respectful to his classmates and focused on his work. That's greatness!"

Variations on this game are only limited by your creativity. Instead of revealing the name of the mystery student, you might give greatness clues all day long about the student who was chosen. Get more specific as the day goes on; by the end of the day, the class will be able to pick the mystery child out based on the qualities of greatness he or she was "accused" of reflecting. Once his or her fellow students are ready to guess the identity of the mystery student, let them give it a shot; then, let them energize him some more. "Let's tell on Mario!

What irrefutable evidence do we have of his greatness?" Let students offer evidence. "He's a great rule follower, a great friend!" This game really helps get everyone motivated!

Machan Magnificents

At Machan School in Phoenix, Arizona, students have access to note cards that they can fill out with callouts about others' greatness. The cards are put into a fish bowl at a central location. Each day, the principal reads a couple of these cards over the PA system. Cards will often start out with, "(Name) was magnificent because..." I've been at Machan during morning announcements, and I've seen kids in the middle of their busy mornings drop everything and become completely silent to hear about the magnificence of their peers.

Greatness Growth Charts

In preschool and kindergarten, teachers will sometimes maintain growth charts with each child's picture. The child's height is measured periodically and recorded. On the other side of the chart, records are added of the ways in which the child grew in greatness since last being measured. At parent-teacher conferences, these charts are excellent conversation starters around each child's greatness which, in this approach, is the main topic to address at these conferences!

Me-You-Superstar

This is a game I like to play in one-day trainings. I put three pieces of paper into a coffee can: one says, "ME," one says, "YOU," and the other says, "SUPERSTAR." Each person takes a turn picking a paper:

- ✓ Those who pick "ME" get to recognize themselves for their own greatness.
- ✓ Those who pick "YOU" give a compliment to the person on their right.
- ✓ Those who pick "SUPERSTAR" get to go into the middle of the circle to be energized by everyone else!

It s possible to play this game with 20 people in 20 minutes, and it works with any age—kindergarteners through high schoolers and beyond. A round of Me-You-Superstar can be played any time a strong dose of emotional nutrition is called for. Rhett Etherton often uses this game in his Greatness Circle for educators.

Greatness Circles

A simplified but no less powerful version of Me-You-Superstar. Sit in a circle and tell students that you're going to take some time to talk about the greatness of you and me, and to explore what greatness means. Then, take turns energizing one another and yourselves. These circles are a place where Nurtured Heart language can be practiced, and where students, teachers or administrators are immersed in the culture of the approach.

Time to Tell On

Set your timer for 10 minutes. Allow students to raise a hand if they want to "tell on" someone (for their greatness). You can also draw names: one student to tell on another, and a second student to be told on.

What's Going Well

This is a structured way for teachers to "broadcast" what's going right in the classroom. In traditional teaching, teachers are taught not to interrupt the learning process; here, you get really animated when students are focused. Interrupt them. Say what's going well, then go back to what you are doing.

This creates a climate of self-motivation, confidence, and self-worth. Regular doses of emotional nutrition are offered. Think of it as "drip irrigation"—there's a constant drip, drip, drip throughout the day as students are reminded of their greatness in ordinary moments.

Secret Stunning Student

If a child is struggling to fit in or is always in trouble, shift the dynamic proactively to pull the kid in from the fringes. Announce that this student is the day's "Secret Stunning Student" and energize him or her. (Be sure to do this at a time when the student is not acting out.) Invite his or her peers to offer energizing statements as well.

Phone Home In the Moment

Add the phone number of every parent in your classroom to your cell phone. Then, make an occasional habit of calling a student's parents while you're in the flow of teaching...to share about that student's greatness as it's happening!

Notes Home

Teachers can also make a habit of writing home about a student's greatness. Principals can also write notes to teachers or other staff to call them out for being great.

Caught In the Act

This experiential exercise was developed in a central Phoenix school with a strong gang culture where it was considered cool to be bad and those with parents in prison felt more powerful. Teachers hung a mug shot wall outside the vice principal's office, where they hung pictures of identified 'badass' kids doing great things: helping, playing ball, sweeping.

Random Acts of Greatness

Many schools count the first 100 days and celebrate the 100-day mark. You can gear this toward creation of inner wealth by challenging them to do 100 acts of kindness or greatness at home or school. Have them record these acts and describe how they are passing their greatness along and creating a greatness culture in their schools and at home. In keeping track of this as an assignment, students feel more encouraged to do these acts anonymously and they then feel the joy of working to grow greatness all around them!

A variation on this is Pay it Forward, which is based on a website called payitforward.org (and the film by the same name). Talk with students about how many people they can help by helping five people, who then help five more, and so on. You might create some coupons that students can hand to another person they're helping, to say: "Let's see how you can pay it forward."

Nurtured Heart Video Modeling: *For Kids on the Autism Spectrum*

Special Education teacher Linda Grey was working with a child with severe Asperger's. The child would become overstimulated during every transition getting off the bus, changing classrooms, going to the playground and each instance of overstimulation led to a meltdown.

Linda videotaped his entire day and edited out the meltdowns. She then showed the child the edited version of his day, in which he had no meltdowns and was successful! Watching this repeatedly supported the child in believing that he could manage his energy. This was a brilliant way to apply the Nurtured Heart approach with a nonverbal child who needs to work on social skills and with coping with transitions.

A Day In the Life of Julio

This is an exercise that powerfully teaches students how differently positive and negative statements affect them and others, both in the giving of such statements and in receiving them.

The group gathers and one student becomes Julio. He stands in the center of the group and either reads a card with negative self-talk written on it (for example, "I guess I'm a bad kid. I get in trouble all the time. Other kids don't like me, and neither do my teachers. I'm stupid; I don't get math, or English, or science") or have the student improvise these kinds of statements. Then, a few students read cards with negative statements like, "Julio, you're in trouble again!" and "Julio, is that what you're wearing? You look like a hoodlum!" and "Julio, you're going to get sent to the principal."

Then, have other students make positive, energizing statements, where they find positive ways to 'hold up the mirror' to Julio.

Kids really get this. They feel the energetic shift. It helps them to understand the value of this approach; to recognize that so many of their interactions with adults are around negativity, and to feel the difference it makes to have a positive reflection. This makes them want to follow the rules, do better academically, and foster positive relationships.

Peer Mentoring: Cooley's "Greatness Kids"

So much research has been done on peer mentoring and peer support. Peer relationship becomes more important as children grow up; as anyone who works with teens knows, it eventually eclipses primary family relationships in importance. These relationships, in large part, form who children become.

Many schools invest in anti-bullying programs, and these programs are rarely as effective as hoped. They feed the exact fire they are trying to put out! What if the hours spent talking about anti-bullying, which are hours spent energizing the negative, were spent talking about greatness? How can we feed the fire we *want* to feed?

Schools have begun to use the Nurtured Heart Approach to teach students how to interact in ways that build inner wealth. Bullying falls away and the power and intensity that lead to bullying flow in a positive direction.

At Cooley Middle School in Roseville, California, an exemplary peer mentoring program is teaching the Nurtured Heart Approach to students who mentor other students in academic subjects. Celeste Elsey, a special education teacher at Cooley, was instrumental in creating this program. The story, in her words:

At Cooley, many students in Special Ed don't have a way to get to school early or stay late to get extra support. We had to figure out a way to provide it within the school day, and we did this by creating a period four days a week, 29 minutes per day. We called it "E Period" (E stands for "Excel"). Diagnostic tests helped us figure out whether to place a student in an enrichment class (reserved for those without learning issues) or an intervention class (where students who needed extra support could get it). Stephanie Rule, our school counselor, had the idea of placing peer mentors in the intervention E-period classrooms, and to train them in the Nurtured Heart Approach to prepare them to help their peers. Kids who became E-period mentors (later called "Greatness Kids" by Howard Glasser) were those who had high scores on standardized (STAR) tests who had a grasp of the academic material sufficient to help their peers.

When we begin the program each year, we gather 70 to 120 of these mentors for a talk from our principal, Karen Calkins. She explains to them the difference they are making in giving academic support to their peers. They do activities, including filling out worksheets where they list strengths they possess that will help with academic mentoring and doing partner sharing about these strengths. At a subsequent training, they get a 20-minute presentation on the approach: they learn a little about Howard Glasser, about what the approach is, and about the concepts of inner wealth and "Shamu." This always opens up incredible discussions about the value of refusing to energize the negative and recognizing or creating the positive. Peer mentors know that teachers will handle clarity of rules and consequences, but we teach them resets in the context of staying positive with their peers by resetting themselves as often as necessary.

Kids get this stuff so fast. They readily grasp the concept of inner wealth. They get how hearing one negative thing in a day can ruin that whole day, while hearing one positive thing can make the day great. They get to experience the joy of resetting themselves when they feel like gossiping, or saying something unkind, or getting frustrated with a peer who does not accept their help. Middle-school kids don't yet have a background of believing that children need to hear about what they're doing wrong, and the shift to greatness thinking feels right and easy for them.

At the end of the year, all the Greatness Kids receive certificates acknowledging the effort they've made. This program is in its third year at this writing.

Notching it Up!

Brainstorm some ways you might use the Nurtured Heart Approach in a peer mentoring capacity.

Staff Greatness Exercises

From Rhett Etherton:

Anyone who has ever tried to teach nouns to a group of 6th graders on a late Friday afternoon knows that teaching is challenging and draining. Fully implementing the Nurtured Heart Approach requires not only that staff members energize students, but also that staff members energize each other to help get each other through the challenging days.

Try these techniques to improve staff morale:

- ✓ *Nurtured Heart Coffees: This activity contains the two things teachers need most: coffee and being recognized by peers! In the mornings before school at a local coffee shop, participants share with each other what they appreciate about them and why they are a great teacher. The format changes each time: sometimes we play Me-You-Superstar, or sometimes each participant energizes him or herself for one thing and then others energize them around that same thing. Teachers told me that this is the best way to start the day! Try Nurtured Heart Happy Hours to mix things up.*
- ✓ *Greatness Grub Potlucks: Once a week, a Nurtured Heart Connections Teacher group gets together for lunch. People take turns bringing a potluck meal, serving the meal and honoring each person in the group with active greatness energizing or some other theme on perpetuating greatness as a group or within the context of changing school climate.*

- ✓ *Surprise Energizing: With a group of staff members, pick one teacher a month to surprise at their classroom door after school. Each teacher takes a turn telling the chosen teacher why the school is lucky to have them. Bring a sign with an encouraging message and balloons to make it even more of a celebration. One teacher who was selected said she would never forget being surprised with her greatness.*
- ✓ *E-mail Energizing: E-mail your coworkers and ask them to fill up a certain teacher's inbox on a specific day with emails telling them the reasons why they are a hero at the school. Imagine how it feels to receive numerous e-mails like this at every e-mail inbox check throughout the day!*

Notching it Up!

Come up with a few of your own ideas for energizing coworkers.

____

____

____

____

____

____

The ideas in this chapter represent only a few of the ways in which educators have creatively integrated the Nurtured Heart Approach into the flow of their classrooms. Consider them a springboard for your own brilliance!

Chapter Ten

Notching it Up: Summary and Expansion

Integration of the Nurtured Heart Approach tends to happen in layers. First, foundational pieces shift mindset and encourage a heart-centered attitude; then, techniques give tools for creating a vibrant time-in. And finally, the reset adds the balancing third Stand to the first two.

Most who adopt the approach find that they cycle through deepening levels of understanding as they apply it. As Rhett says in his Foreword, there is always a way to take the approach to new levels by "adding more heart to recognitions, becoming...clear about rules and consistent about consequences, and ensuring that all...energy has been reallocated from misbehavior to greatness."

This deepening process is what we call *notching it up:* taking the approach up a step in intensity and heart-centeredness, and continuing to do so until you have the impact you desire. It's about maintaining integrity, power and control through positivity, no matter what chaotic influences threaten to derail you. When you choose to notch it up in the face of resistance, you demonstrate steadfast refusal to be mostly available for problems, drama, misbehavior and chaos. When you relentlessly notch up the positives, you eventually reach a level that transforms your most difficult students and ultimately benefit every child in your classroom.

Before we part, let's recap some of the ways you might notch it up as you 'graduate' from this initial introduction to the Nurtured Heart Approach. (A more detailed discussion of each of these strategies can be found in Glasser and Block's *Notching Up the Nurtured Heart Approach.*)

The exercises in this chapter won't include writing components. They're designed more as experiential pieces to apply as you go through your day. We've included a few blank writing pages in the back of this book just in case you would like to write about these pieces or about anything else you've learned here.

Notch it up by:

Accepting that greatness is your ground truth and the ground truth of everyone around you.

Any expression of positive values, behaviors, traits and choices is an expression of this inherent greatness. Name and celebrate them in yourself and in others at every opportunity. Notice how this creates more of what you want in your life and in your classroom.

Try this: Make a commitment to affirm this ground truth to yourself several times a day—in particular, in the morning upon rising and just before going to bed.

Grounding into your heart when giving recognitions.

Giving recognitions as described in Chapters Four and Five can feel awkward at first. You might struggle to find words that feel right, make sense, and don't energize the negative. Respond to this by sinking your awareness into your heart center.

Try this: Any time you feel yourself in this struggle, pause and focus on your heart center. Take a breath (or a few) into that place. Let whatever emotions and words come up guide you in the next moments.

Shifting from a "good vs. bad" perspective to a greatness perspective.

According to the good vs. bad paradigm, if students are being good, the opposite is always a possibility. This fear of things going south often creates exactly the situations we wish to avoid. A shift to a greatness paradigm helps us see anything that could go wrong as an energy that can be played with and notched up.

Try this: Any time you catch yourself judging something as good or bad, try letting go of that dichotomy. Find greatness instead.

Committing to remain positive and refusing to energize the negative, *no matter what*.

Expect even celebrate resistance as evidence that you are having an impact. Remember: no matter how tough, resistant, defiant or distant the kid, the way through is notching it up.

Try this: When circumstances conspire to derail you, or when you think you have questions about the approach that you can't answer for yourself, make a commitment to remain positive **as though your life depended on it.**

Cultivating clarity.

When the approach isn't working, notch it up by getting more clear about the rules.

Try this: When faced with a tough kid or a tough situation, channel any frustration into more clearly defining the boundary between a rule followed and a rule broken. Pour more energy into energizing students who follow the

rules and give resets every time a rule is broken.

Cultivating fearlessness.

Notching it up requires fearlessness. You'll feel fear, because everyone does, but you don't have to let fear make your decisions for you. Be fearless about staying in the present instead of entertaining fear about the future or regrets about the past. Be fearless about your refusal to energize the negative and to be relentless with the positives like a dog with a bone.

This will support you in implementing a cultural shift in your classroom that may, at times, feel unpredictable, unusual, or uncomfortable. The more comfortable you are with feeling uncomfortable, the more you will understand the emotional needs of your students as you fearlessly redefine the culture of your classroom.

Try this: Practice fearlessness. Energize yourself any time you notice yourself living fearlessly.

Shifting critical thinking to greatness thinking; resetting yourself as often as necessary.

Whenever you catch yourself thinking critically, reframe problem orientation to a greatness mindset. Accept that this resetting process is part of the game of flipping energy right side up. Note any tendency to default to a traditional, punitive framework; then, bless and release.

Try this: Reset yourself every time you fall into a critical or self-critical mode. Channel the energy that would have gone toward the negative into cultivating greatness in the next moment. Refuse to energize your self-critical inner voice. Notice that when you energize what you do want instead of what you don't want, problems start to solve themselves.

Applying the approach to every student.

Avoid selectively applying the approach to your "high rollers." It works best for them, and for every student, when applied equally over the entire class. A whole-school approach is better yet.

Try this: Deliver energizing statements to every student you encounter, from the high roller to the kid who seems never to have broken a rule in his life. Let them each hear you energizing the other.

Embracing resistance.

See resistance as energy waiting to be channeled in a different direction. Use resets to guide the energy of resistance into success. Cumulative, consistent experiences of being "handled" successfully guide the resistant child to a recognition that a life lived in greatness is more rewarding than the alternative.

When a child tries to wrangle you into relationship around negativity, silently acknowledge any anger or frustration you feel. Acknowledge yourself for handling it well, then *use that energy* to move both you and that child back to time-in. On the outside, remain emotionally neutral until it's time to welcome the high-roller back to time-in.

Try this: Next time you're stumped by whatever is transpiring in your classroom, check in with your feelings. Experience them as pure energy, then consciously channel that energy into more positivity. Reset yourself as often as necessary.

Taking excellent care of yourself.

If you are anything like the educators we know, you eat, sleep and breathe your calling. You teach, organize, and supervise everywhere you go: your front yard, church, a friend's birthday party.

Being an educator requires a thick skin and a lot of heart...it is *not* for the meek or mild! And this approach asks a lot of you, but it gives a lot back, too. Self-care, self-forgiveness and self-love are important ingredients in the Nurtured Heart mix not just in your students, but in you.

Try this: Actively cultivate self-care. Eat well, exercise, and get plenty of rest. When you forget to take excellent care of yourself, reset by engaging in self-care in some small way. Open up to receiving love and help from the people around you.

Using the approach on yourself.

Now that you have gained a high level of expertise in this approach, *use it on yourself.* Fan the flames of your own greatness. Use the language of the approach with friends, partners and coworkers and let it come back to you. Stand in your greatness whenever you can. You don't need problems to create relationship with your students, and you don't need them to create relationship with yourself, either.

This may be the most important notch-it-up secret: *it's much harder to shine light on others' greatness without an equal willingness to shine it on your own.* Greatness doesn't belong to any one person. It's the subtext, the substrate of being human, and we all get to share in it.

Try this: Go deeper, pixelate, go up a level, notch it up however you wish to describe the process of finding more to nurture and celebrate in yourself and others. There's no limit. Absolutely no limit!

To your greatness! —*Lisa and Howie*

Resources

Nurtured Heart Approach Support Information

THREE WEBSITES are available to those who seek further information about the Nurtured Heart Approach: www.childrenssuccessfoundation.com and www.difficultchild.com

The Children's Success Foundation website is the online learning center for the Nurtured Heart Approach. It is a website where parents, educators, coaches and therapists gain quick acquisition of the approach techniques and then continually hone their expertise through innovative learning modules, discussion forums, web courses as well as feature articles, products and services supporting the approach.

The Difficult Child website is also fully in support of learning the Nurtured Heart Approach and providing an array of resources.

Books on the Nurtured Heart Approach

Those listed below are available in most libraries and bookstores and from online sources. They can also be ordered at the Nurtured Heart Approach websites, www.difficultchild.com or www.nurturinggreatness.net, or via a toll free call to 800-311-3132.

Transforming the Difficult Child: The Nurtured Heart Approach (Revised 2008) by Howard Glasser and Jennifer Easley

All Children Flourishing – Igniting the Greatness of Our Children (2008) by Howard Glasser with Melissa Lynn Block

Transforming the Difficult Child Workbook – An Interactive Guide to the Nurtured Heart Approach (2008) by Howard Glasser, Joann Bowdidge and Lisa Bravo.

The Inner Wealth Initiative – The Nurtured Heart Approach for Educators (2007) by Howard Glasser and Tom Grove with Melissa Lynn Block.

You Are Oprah – Igniting the Fires of Greatness (2009) by Howard Glasser with Melissa Lynn Block

ADHD Without Drugs – A Guide to the Natural Care of Children with ADHD (2010) – Sanford Newmark, MD

Transforming the Difficult Child: True Stories of Triumph (2008) by Howard Glasser and Jennifer Easley

Notching Up the Nurtured Heart Approach – The New Inner Wealth Initiative for Educators (2011) Howard Glasser and Melissa Lynn Block

Audio Visual Resources

Transforming the Difficult Child DVD – (2004) 6 Hours based on an actual filmed one-day seminar – with video clip illustrations.

Transforming the Difficult Child DVD – (2004) 4 Hours based on an abbreviated version of the above.

Transforming the Difficult Child CD – (2011) 3.5 Hours recorded from a live seminar.

Transforming the Difficult Child: The Nurtured Heart Approach – Audio Book (2012) – by Howard Glasser and Jennifer Easley – Read by Howard Glasser.

About the Authors

Lisa Bravo

Co-Executive Director of the Children's Success Foundation

LISA BRAVO, MC, LPC, LISAC, is a Certified Nurtured Heart Trainer of Trainers. She brings together over 20 years of experience in the areas of parenting coaching, mental health counseling, crisis and chemical dependency interventions, consultations, and training to her counseling and consulting practice, ParentwoRx. The majority of her time is spent helping families, schools, and agencies implement the Nurtured Heart Approach. She is a proud mother of two and is raising her children based on the principles of the Nurtured Heart Approach.

Lisa is Co-Executive Director of The Children's Success Foundation and co-author of the top-selling *Nurtured Heart Workbook* (2007). Lisa has trained thousands of educators, clinicians, professionals, and parents at the Advanced Nurtured Heart Approach Certification Trainings held throughout the year.

Howard Glasser

Executive Director of the Children's Success Foundation & Creator of The Nurtured Heart Approach

HOWARD GLASSER IS THE FOUNDER of the Children's Success Foundation and creator of the Nurtured Heart Approach™, which has been used in hundreds of thousands of homes and classrooms around the world.

He is author of *Transforming the Difficult Child*, currently the top-selling book on the topic of ADHD and otherwise challenging children; *The Inner Wealth Initiative*, one of the leading books on school interventions; *You Are Oprah – Igniting the Fires of Greatness*, a book that outlines ways to apply the Nurtured Heart Approach to one's self; and *All Children Flourishing*, a book that describes the approach's use with all children, difficult or not. Four of his eight books are in the top one percent of all books on **Amazon.com**

Howard has been a featured guest on CNN and a consultant for 48 Hours. He currently teaches the Nurtured Heart Approach through live presentations worldwide. He has consulted for numerous psychiatric, judicial and educational programs.

Howard has been called one of the most influential living persons working to prevent children from relying on psychiatric medications. His work also supports many children in developing the inner strength to resist addictive substances.

Although he has done extensive doctoral work in the fields of Clinical Psychology and Educational Leadership, he feels his own years as a difficult child contributed the most to his understanding of the needs of challenging children and to the success of his approach, which is based on aligning the energies of relationship.

Melissa Lynn Block, M.Ed.

Melissa Block is a freelance writer, editor, yoga student and teacher, and non-profit development professional who has contributed to eight books on the Nurtured Heart Approach. She has been a Nurtured Heart Approach Advanced Trainer since 2009. She lives in Santa Barbara, California with her two children, Sarah and Noah Block.

Notching it Up!

Notching it Up!

Notching it Up!

Notching it Up!

Notching it Up!

Ways to Earn	Points	Ways to Spend	Points